CORSAIRS &
FREEBOOTERS

A Collection of Pungent Remarks

In the War of Ideas

Edward Cline

Patrick Henry Press

Library of Congress Cataloguing-in-Publication Data

Edward Cline (1946 -)
Corsairs and Freebooters/Edward Cline

ISBN 978-1481804509

Cover Illustration: The U.S.S. *Enterprise* Capturing the Tripolitan Corsair *Tripoli*, 1 August 1801. From a drawing (circa 1878) by Captain William Bainbridge Hoff, U.S. Navy, in the collection of the Navy Department.

Patrick Henry Press
Williamsburg, VA

Publisher's Note: This book is a collection of essays published on Rule of Reason, blog site for the Center for the Advancement of Capitalism, and in other venues. These essays are copyrighted by the author.

Table of Contents

Foreword

Foreword

In this third anthology of commentaries and essays, all of which have been published on one blog site or another, often in multiple venues, I focus chiefly on Islam and its depredations, methods, irrationality, and seemingly ineluctable advance in its intended conquest of the West, including the United States. This advance is enabled by that philosophical version of the Four Horsemen of the Apocalypse – altruism, pragmatism, subjectivism, and multiculturalism – that informs and governs Western policies. Too often, more perceptive and anxious men are astonished by the suicidal nature of these policies, believing that their practitioners are only acting out of ignorance, that "they do not know what they do," and are willing to forgive these policymakers by presuming that it is only an error of knowledge that can be corrected by pointing out the debilitating and destructive consequences of those policies.

They are disarmed by a common disbelief that the consequences are intentional. The only weapon left to them then is outrage at the irrational and the evil, without examining the fact that the consciously irrational is fundamentally evil, and that the practitioners know "without knowing" what they are doing. In such a battle for freedom, one becomes exasperated with such moral and intellectual allies, and more of one's anger is often directed at them and not at the evil-doers.

Three articles focus on the thuggish progeny of the Four Horsemen, the aimless, shapeless manqués of Occupy Wall Street. Since their appearance last Fall they have virtually monopolized headlines and behaved with all the violence and arrogance of Nazi Brownshirts. Indeed, since many of their "campsites" in public parks and other places have finally been cleaned out, they seem to have formed flying squads of protestors and gangs around the country dedicated to interrupting or stopping any event that displeases them. They have announced on their website their plans to oppose those events with noise, chanting, chaos, vandalism, trespass, and physical violence.

The last trio of articles dwells on the Clintons, one a frustrated frump and pathetic vestige of a woman, the other a stealthy but shrewd kingmaker whose past policies have simply been expanded and honed by the Obama administration. Both have been wined and dined by the Four Horsemen, and also by the Mainstream Media, that tribe of harpies and political paparazzi dominated by the Left.

Long Live Lady Liberty.

Edward Cline
Williamsburg, Virginia
February 2012

The Black Flag of Islamic Jihad

Islam

Barbary Pirates: Old and New

"The Policy of Christendom has made Cowards of all their Sailors before the Standard of Mahomet. It would be heroical and glorious in Us, to restore Courage to ours. I doubt not we could accomplish it, if we should set about it in earnest. But the Difficulty of bringing our People to agree upon it, has ever discouraged me."*

So wrote John Adams to Thomas Jefferson, ministers of the United States to Britain and France respectively, in 1786, expressing their mutual distaste for having to pay the Barbary pirates to stop seizing American merchant vessels in the Mediterranean and enslaving their crews and/or holding them for ransom. By "Christendom" he meant most of the European powers, which simply paid tribute to the pirates to leave their merchant vessels alone.

Adams himself proposed paying the bribe in order to allow American traders to sail the Mediterranean unmolested, reasoning that, in terms of money, the amount of trade possible there would far outweigh any "Sum of Money" paid to the pirates. He proposed that, not out of pragmatism, but because he doubted that "our People" – meaning Congress – would be willing to approve a navy that would punish the pirates and protect American ships.

For Adams and Jefferson, it was a matter of finding the money to build and sustain such a navy. Even when America had a navy, its merchant vessels remained the prey of not only Islamic pirates, but were harassed or obstructed.

1

by British and French navies, as well, a practice that with Britain led to another war, and near-war with France. Adding to their frustrations was an ineffectual Congress hamstrung by war debt and the anemic Articles of Confederation, not to mention civil unrest that culminated in Shay's Rebellion in Massachusetts.

And Congress had authorized only $80,000 with which to bargain with all the Barbary States, not nearly enough to satiate the looting appetites of a single one of them. And this money could be had only on credit – from loans to the U.S. by principally Dutch bankers. For example, the "Bashaws" of the Barbary States had various "sliding scales" of prisoner ransom values, say, from $300 for a common seaman to $1,000 or more for a ship's captain.

This would have been in addition to a substantial flat purchase price, the exorbitant commission and expenses demanded by an Islamic "ambassador" or negotiating party for deigning to discuss the matter, and spectacular "presents" to the ruler of a Barbary nation as a gesture of "good will," all of it in cash. (These amounts were in real money, that is, gold and silver.)

Adams and Jefferson were at the time attempting to conduct negotiations with the Algerian Dey with envoys authorized by Congress for that purpose. But even if they had managed to "treat" successfully with Algiers and paid the tribute, there remained the Deys, Beys and Pashas of Tunis and Tripoli to placate, not to mention the Porte, or the Sultan of Turkey in Constantinople, whose pirates also raided the Mediterranean. A treaty of "peace" with one would not necessarily mean an end to the others' depredations. (A treaty with Morocco was ratified by Congress in July, 1786.) And there were no guarantees that any of the Barbary "regencies" would not renege on a treaty and resume its raiding. They all knew that the U.S. had no way of enforcing the terms of a treaty or of retaliating if the terms were violated.

In a letter of July 3, 1786, to Jefferson in Paris, Adams outlined his "premises" concerning the dilemma:

1. *We may at this Time, have a Peace with them* [the Barbary pirates], *in spite of all the Intrigues of the English or others to prevent it, for a Sum of Money.*

2. *We never Shall have Peace, though France, Spain, England, and Holland Should use all their Influence in our favor without a Sum of Money.*

3. *That neither the Benevolence of France nor the Malevolence of England will be ever able materially to diminish or Increase the Sum.*

4. *The longer the Negotiation is delayed, the larger will be the Demand.*

Jefferson was more adamant concerning the Barbary pirates, preferring to send a squadron of American warships to the Mediterranean to deal permanently with the corsairs. In his reply to Adams of July 11, after conceding the "practical" wisdom of paying tribute, he wrote:

> *I acknowledge I very early thought it would be best to effect a peace through the medium of war....I should prefer the obtaining* [of] *it by war.*
>
> 1. *Justice is in favor of this opinion.*
> 2. *Honor favors it.*
> 3. *It will procure us respect in Europe, and respect is a safeguard to interest.*
> 4. *It will arm the federal head with the safest of all the instruments of coercion over their delinquent members and prevent them from using what would be less safe.*
> 5. *I think it least expensive.*
> 6. *Equally effectual.*

But, the conundrum was insoluble for as long as the U.S. government lacked the will and the means to act. It had no "instrument of coercion." The Continental navy of the Revolution had been disbanded. The only country that offered America any assistance was Portugal, which in 1786 ordered its navy to protect American merchantmen at the Strait of Gibraltar. Jefferson further proposed to Adams the idea of a naval alliance between the U.S., Portugal, and Naples (then capital of the kingdom of the Two Sicilies) to confront the Barbary nations and end their outrages. Nothing came of it. All the European diplomats on speaking terms with Jefferson and Adams advised that the U.S. pay the tribute.

While Jefferson remained in Paris as minister, he made arrangements with the Catholic Order of Mathurins, which had for centuries begged alms with which to buy the freedom of chiefly Frenchmen taken captive by the Barbary pirates. The head of the order agreed to try to redeem as many Americans as he could, especially from the Algerians. Before enough funds could be collected, however, the French Revolution occurred and the new, anti-cleric government dissolved the Mathurins.

Treaties were signed between the U.S. and all the Barbary States in the late 18th century, but these more or less lapsed when the British navy barred American merchantmen from the Mediterranean during the War of 1812. With the end of the Napoleonic Wars in 1815, together with the treaty between the U.S. and Britain the same year, the Barbary States again felt free to raid American vessels.

The United States Navy was created by an act of Congress on April 30, 1798. Between 1805 and 1815, under Jefferson's and Madison's administrations, the Navy and its Marines solved the problem, restoring Adams' "Courage" to the American standard.

The moral of this narrative is that while Americans, particularly Jefferson and Adams, held the rational moral principle regarding the proper way to deal with the Barbary States – with retaliatory force – they lacked the means. But when they had the means, they acted on that principle. The European powers, on the other hand, particularly Britain, France and Spain, possessed the "instruments of coercion" – large and powerful navies – but chose instead to submit to Moslem extortion in policies of craven pragmatism.

It was not until the U.S. took the moral "high ground" that European nations abandoned their "pragmatic sanction." For example, British admiral Exmouth, commanding an Anglo-Dutch fleet, reduced Algiers in 1816 when it reneged on the treaty it made with American commodore Stephen Decatur the year before, and forced the Dey to sign a second treaty that reaffirmed Decatur's terms.

Today, the U.S., in addition to the West, is being raided and plundered and held hostage by a new gang of Barbary States – Saudi Arabia, Iran, Syria, and even our "ally" Pakistan, not to mention all the oligarchical/feudal Gulf States now thriving on seized Western oil assets. No nation, not even the U.S., can agree on the proper action to take against them, or whether any action would be proper. This is because they lack, not the "instruments of coercion," but rather the moral courage to assert their selfish existence.

Jefferson almost had it right when he nearly said, in reply to Adams in 1786, that the rationally moral is the practical.

The Adams-Jefferson Letters: The Complete Correspondence between Thomas Jefferson and Abigail and John Adams (Chapel Hill: University of North Carolina Press, 1959). Ed. Lester J. Cappon. All of the quotations and most of the information in this commentary come from this work. Also, complete texts of all the treaties with the Barbary States are available at Yale Law School's Avalon Project site.

August 2007

Western Reason vs. Islamic Mysticism

A "moderate" Muslim organization called "Muslims Against Sharia" commented on my "Islamophobia is Justified" commentary (in English and in Swedish, no less) on the Rule of Reason blogsite. Here is my reply to it. I do no often respond to criticisms by Muslims, but the reader will see why I do in this instance in the first and last paragraphs.

Sirs/Mesdames:

Thank you for replying to my "Islamophobia is Justified" commentary on Rule of Reason. It quite startled me that you not only praised the Swedish cartoonist Lars Vilks and his colleagues, but also countered with your own bounty on the head of Abu Omar Al Baghdadi (obviously an alias of the contrivance of the coward who hides behind it).

I printed out your Muslims against Sharia Manifesto to read more closely and to compose some commentary on it. You are to be commended for taking the position on Sharia law that you have – that it must be completely abolished – and I agree with many of the points in the Manifesto, if not entirely with their style of expression, then in spirit, especially in regard to religious privacy, outdated practices, words and phrases, and especially with your endorsement of free expression in terms of depicting Mohammad. I particularly liked your characterization of terrorists as "homicidal zombies'; a more accurate description of them I have not encountered elsewhere.

All that, together with your condemnation of Muslims who murder Muslims and non-Muslims in the name of Islam, certainly deserves recognition of your courage and honesty, and you have mine.

You posed a very interesting question in the Manifesto. After citing the possible (and likely) corruption of the Bible over the centuries (if not expedient inventions of great parts of it by the Church), you ask: "Could it be possible that the *Koran* itself was corrupted by Muslims over the last thirteen centuries?"

I'm sure you are aware of the abrogation issue concerning the *Koran*, and if you or Muslim scholars attempt to reform Islam, this will be a major and I think insurmountable hurdle. It is my understanding that the earlier sections of the *Koran* and Hadith reveal a sort of "kinder, gentler" Mohammad who did not call for war against all unbelievers. I would probably agree with some historians who aver that these sections were calculated merely to win him allies among non-Muslims during his campaign to conquer the Arabian Peninsula. There is no other accounting for their content other than that they are a form of taqiya. Later sections of the *Koran* abrogate or supplant the earlier ones, however, and these contain the homicidal and belligerent injunctions that fundamentalists cite to sanction jihad.

Another issue I think you or your scholars would face would be retaining Islam's purported "peaceful" identity, so reforming it would prove to be a daunting but nevertheless insoluble and impossible task.

If you performed a theological and textual vivisection on the written corpus of the religion – that is, managed to "reform" it by excising all its objectionable injunctions, leaving only its more "benign" aspects – could you could still call it "Islam"? What would be left would be a collection of unconnected, disparate rules and sentiments with no system at all. It might be a more pacific creed, akin to the Amish or Quaker, but would it still retain the identity you wanted to preserve? I don't think it would. You would need to call it by another name.

My final remarks concern faith. Muslims, like Christians, Jews and other religionists, have "faith" in the existence of a supreme being, and that what such a being commands or prescribes as moral is true and right. Of this, all religionists are "certain."

Now, there is a crucial difference between faith and certainty. You exhibit certainty about the existence, for example, of your car keys, that the laws of cause and effect will enable you to unlock the car door with them, and that the laws of physics will cause them to start the engine. Your certainty is grounded in reality. You don't even think about it, or need to think about it. Reality and your certainty about it are the given.

You exhibit faith when you believe, without so much as an iota of proof, in the existence of a supernatural being who has never appeared to anyone in history, but whose existence is merely asserted by priests, mullahs or other professional mystics. Apocryphal anecdotes about this being comprise all the sacred texts of all the religions, all of them claiming at some point that this being spoke to or appeared before or somehow manifested his existence to a variety of prophets, seers, saints and so on.

But all of these assertions are merely legends that offer no supporting evidence to substantiate them other than what long-dead, shadowy monks and the like recorded. A pile of unsubstantiated written assertions does not make a truth, no matter how many millions of words or thousands of pages are devoted to "proving" it. Nor do millions of people believing in a thing make it a fact or a truth.

But, you are asked (or told) to accept this "truth" on faith. In short, you are expected to treat the unreal as real. Further, you are not permitted to think about or doubt or question what you are expected to believe. You are not to apply reason to the subject. Even further, you are expected, under pain of sin or punishment, to conduct your life according to a chaos of arbitrary rules and injunctions – pacific or not – purportedly authored by a being – call him Allah, God, Siva, Brahma, Vishnu, or Wontonka – evidence of whose existence you have not a shred, except for the assertions or say-so of a hierarchy of witch doctors.

As you have probably concluded, I am an atheist. I was raised in the Catholic faith, but I could never take it seriously, because every one of its tenets contradicted the evidence of my senses and my nature as a thinking, volitional being, and my senses and my mind and my nature are engineered to deal with reality, not with some fictive other-worldly realm. Every human being is so engineered, without exception, and nature did the engineering or "designing," not a ghost. If reason cannot be applied to an issue, in this instance, the existence of a supreme being, call him what you will, if it is excluded from any discussion of the subject, then I see no reason to concern myself with the question.

But, you might ask, as so many Christians and Jews do, what about the "first cause"? What about the "beginning"? The cosmologies of the various religions, including Islam's, are ludicrous, fantastic and metaphysically impossible. I think that most men suffer from a kind of mental block, or absorb it from our semi-rational culture, that stops them from accepting the axiom that existence exists. Period. So they become nominally "faithful" or agnostic.

The concept of a "first cause" or "beginning" is a logical fallacy that beggars metaphysical validation, and is subject to an endless reductio ad absurdum argument. Did existence come into existence when Allah or God or Vishnu snapped his fingers or just "wished" it, and if existence didn't exist before that, where did this being reside if matter and nothingness did not exist before he did, and where did he come from, and why is his supernatural realm always beyond human perception and comprehension? And so on. It is a matter deserving an essay far longer than my remarks here. Aristotle and Ayn Rand have done a better job of exploding that concept than I could ever attempt.

As a primitive form of philosophy, I do not think any religion is "great." It has caused so much misery, suffering, horror and destruction in man's history. And because it has attracted so much attention lately, I find Islam especially repellent for its degrading rituals, prohibitions and virulent anti-mindedness. I don't like seeing men bowing to a ghost or throwing pebbles at a rock in defiance of another ghost.

Faith and reason are incompatible and antithetical means of living, but most men commit the error of compartmentalizing them to avoid facing the issue. They know that doing the hokey-pokey while reciting a doggerel won't cause their car keys to work, but they'll do much the same thing believing it will make a morality work.

Because your Manifesto exhibited a quantum of reason, as did your response to my Islamophobia commentary, I thought it earned a reciprocal reply, which is the best kind of respect I can offer. However, I do not wish to debate this subject at any length, but hope you accept my observations in the spirit in which they are offered.

Sincerely......

September 2007

Beheading Nations

Veritas, an infant political party in Britain, recently sent an email circular to voters. Its principal subject was the unopposed Islamization of Britain. Addressed to Muslims who are dissatisfied that Britain isn't an Islamic island paradise, the circular suggested that if Muslims don't like the culture, the language, the history, or even other Britons, then they should emigrate or re-emigrate to countries that are more amenable to the strictures of their creed and compatible with their frankly barbaric social customs and ethos (and perhaps even surrender their British passports at the exit door), and not expect all Britons to discard their identities and squeeze into a Mohammedan mould.

I responded that while this was good, reasonable advice, I believed it overlooked an important element in the phenomenon. Muslims will reply to it by cocking a very vile snook. The advice asks Muslims to be reasonable, but they are here, by and large, to conquer and not open to reason. Reason has never been an ally of conquerors. This has been stated repeatedly by their spokesmen, by their clerics, by their muscle, in Britain, and in the hapless nations on the Continent. They are not here to assimilate, to learn the value of freedom, individualism, or capitalism, or the rule of rational law, or to glory in the superiority of Western civilization and to share its fruits.

They are here to help destroy it all (with a great assist from multiculturalism and its advocates in office and out of it, and no one should doubt that they know how to exploit that political solvent). To level it first, and then lord over what's left. They want segregated "no go" areas in which to live in Western countries where neither the police nor national law may intrude or overrule Sharia law and the crimes committed under it.

I recently came across a frightening article, "Beheading Nations: The Islamization of Europe's Cities." It describes in lurid detail the method of Islamic revanchism, bogus as that is. I quote one paragraph of it, to substantiate my claims above:

> "In an online story in the Daily Telegraph that was removed 'for legal reasons,' former Muslim Dr. Patrick Sookhdeo warned that British Muslims could soon form a state within a state. Dr. Sookhdeo believed that 'in a decade, you will see parts of English cities which are controlled by Muslim clerics and which follow, not the common law, but aspects of Muslim Sharia law....In 1980, the Islamic Council of Europe laid out their strategy for the future — and the fundamental rule was never dilute your presence. That is to say, do not integrate....Rather, concentrate Muslim presence in a particular area until you are a majority in that area, so that the institutions of the local community come to reflect Islamic strictures....'"

The "Beheading" article goes on to say: "The next step will be pushing the Government to recognize Sharia law for Muslim communities...." I imagine that the next step would be for venal politicians and jurists to advocate that Sharia law be made coequal with common law, so as to placate "disgruntled" Muslims and not rile them to the point that they would begin rioting French-Muslim style and declaring war on non-Muslims. A government that has surrendered the power to enforce objective law within its legal boundaries is no longer a government. Common law would then be displaced at the point of a gun, town by town, then county by county. Look at Lebanon, whose population is about one-half non-Muslim. Hezbollah rules it, establishes its policies, and makes war. Its parliament is a joke.

Need I say more? I strongly recommend the "Beading" article, written by someone named Fjordman (likely a protective pseudonym). It is packed with sobering facts.

I wonder for what "legal reasons" the Sookhdeo article was removed from the online Telegraph. Did it "offend" someone's sensibilities? Anyway, I can only hope that the Veritas appeal rouses enough Britons to move their representatives to throw back the new Huns, or at least caution them to keep a low profile and stay the hell out of the way of people who want to live on earth. Perhaps if they succeed, the same phenomenon can be nipped in the bud here in the U.S. It is not as advanced a problem here as it is in Britain or in Europe, but moral vacuums invite conquerors to fill them. Patterson, New Jersey, is our own Bradford. Its Muslim population danced in the streets and passed out candy in sight of the rising plumes of smoke from the World Trade Center across the Hudson River.

August 2006

Burning the *Koran* is Self-Defeating

Missing most from arguments against burning *Koran*s is the fact that a *Koran* may be one's personal property. This fact is overlooked in all arguments I have read against the action. It is also absent from the argument that when authorities arrest someone who is charged with a "hate crime," or with "hate speech," or even with "promoting racial hatred," the property status of the book is not considered relevant. It is one's property, but it is subject to the equivalent of a local building or property code on speech.

Burning a book – the *Koran*, the *Bible*, the *Torah*, *Mein Kampf*, *Das Kapital*, *Ulysses*, *Lady Chatterley's Lover*, any of the *Harry Potter* novels, even of *Atlas Shrugged*, or any work that someone or some group may object to – is basically an emotional expression of the contempt , anger, or fear one harbors for the book. It is fundamentally cathartic in nature; it begins with the flames and ends with the ashes. The emotion is indulged and expended, privately or in public. It is certainly a species of freedom of speech, or of expression, but what does it accomplish beyond the satisfaction of having committed the action?

I do not see that it accomplishes anything tangible, except for the declaration of a particular attitude, view, or position, which may or may not be rational, for all to witness and evaluate. Burning a *Koran* lets friends, enemies, and the disinterested know where one stands on a specific issue. If one fears or despises the implementation of the Mohammedan diktats in the *Koran*, one certainly has the right to burn the work in a public or private venue. But one would better contribute to the defeat of the Islamists – who base their stealthy and violent actions on the contents of the *Koran*, and who, to judge by their actions in this country and around the world, should be feared – by writing a critique of Islam.

Burning a *Koran* should not be regarded or treated as a crime or a criminal action. The hate, the speech, the fear, or the bigotry demonstrated in such an action is one's own, not anyone else's, not the government's, not society's. It is a personal affair which one has chosen to make public. Once demonstrated, the hate, the fear, the speech, or the bigotry is in the open for others' evaluations, for better or for worse.

To punish, fine, or otherwise prohibit a person by force from the expression of his own mind, at his own risk, expense, and venue (or even in a "public" place) is to impose politically correct speech, or censorship.

Conversely, "hate speech" statutes not only represent an attempt at thought control, but insulate the "hated" from criticism and opposition, deserved or not. Words, unlike bullets or stones, have no metaphysical attributes to harm, injure, or kill. It is only one's premises that are subject to correction or "wounding."

Several arguments have been made in favor of burning and/or banning of the *Koran*, based on some inexplicable danger it represents. None of them is valid. Geert Wilders, the Dutch politician, for example, courageous as he may be, has called for a ban of the *Koran*, just as Adolf Hitler's *Mein Kampf* has been banned in Germany and in other countries. Wilders has rightfully compared the *Koran* with *Mein Kampf.* Both works are about a "struggle" to implement the authors' world views, which include conquest and the elimination or subjugation of enemies. Both works, he says, are threats in and of themselves.

The *Koran* is anti-Christian. This is true. Unlike the *Bible*, it is a collection of primitive homilies and diktats to Muslims to keep the faith and to spread it, violently if necessary. The *Koran* is most like the Old Testament, all blood and thunder and rapine and conquest of unbelievers and sinners. Somewhat like the Old Testament, it was written by a tribalist for tribalists. It has no place in the modern world. It has as much to do with morality as Indian rain dances have to do with climatology. The Old Testament, however, is balanced by the pacific New Testament. The *Koran* stands by itself, unbalanced by an ancillary or supplementary text, unrepentant in its horrid, barbaric tribalism.

More germane, however, is that the *Koran* is also anti-atheist, anti-gay, anti-woman, anti-Jew, anti-reason, and much, much more. Christians do not have a monopoly on being hated and targeted by Islam through the sanction of the *Koran* for conquest, submission, persecution, or elimination.

The *Koran*, as a moral and political expression of Islam, is un-American. This is true. One could even claim that it is anti-American. It does not advocate individualism, reason, limited government, and freedom of speech, but their opposites: conformity, irrationality, totalitarianism, and censorship. The *Koran* does not at all resonate with the Declaration of Independence or the Constitution.

An article on the Holocaust Museum site about the May 10th, 1933 book-burning in Nazi Germany cites the German students' reasons for participating in the burnings. That event was billed as a "spontaneous" protest against Jewish and "un-German" influences in German culture, orchestrated, however, by the Nazi Party. About the first major book-burning by students in Germany in 1817, the article explains:

> The students, demonstrating for a unified country — Germany was then a patchwork of states — burned anti-national and reactionary texts and literature which the students viewed as "Un-German."

And, writing about the 1933 book-burning:

> The students described the "action" as a response to a worldwide Jewish "smear campaign" against Germany and an affirmation of traditional German values.

Substitute "Jewish" with "Arab," Germany" with "America," "un-German" and "traditional German values" with "un-American" and "traditional American values." What is the meaning of "un-American," and what are "traditional American values"? Other than the conservative, non-intellectual assertion that they are family, home, and religion, I have never read any statement of what those values are.

The *Koran*, like *Mein Kampf*, can seduce men's minds, and so should be banned. The state of Bavaria controls the copyright and publication rights to Hitler's book, whose copyright will expire in 2015. Officials have blocked wishes to have the book republished, citing its possible deleterious influence on certain segments of the German population. The British Daily Mail had an article about the drive to republish *Main Kampf*.

> The Bavarian government do not want Hitler's words to be abused by neo-Nazi. Historians say a thorough, academic presentation that places Hitler's work in historical context would be the best defense against neo-Nazis who might want to use the book to advance racist agendas.

> Bavarian lawmakers have routinely turned down calls to reprint the book for fear that it might be misused by right-wing extremists and out of respect for the victims of the Holocaust.... "Mein Kampf" was banned from publication after World War II. Possession and resale of old copies in Germany is legal, but highly regulated.

This position ascribes to evil – and both works do advocate evil ideas and actions – a potency it does not possess. There is no innate power in either work to magically work its corruption in men's minds. This position views men's minds as passive receptors, and the books as insidious incubi. But a copy of the *Koran*, like a copy of *Mein Kampf*, is merely a collection of atoms. The paper and the ink on it that forms audio-visual symbols that are words are not an alchemist's formulae for turning gold into acid. No combination of words, whatever its content or purpose, can cast an irresistible hex or spell on anyone's mind, neither at a glance nor during years of examination. Philosophies, Ideologies and systems of ideas do not have the power of autosuggestion.

Evil has only the appearance of virility and strength, when in fact it is strong only in proportion to the unwillingness of men to oppose it or acknowledge it. Men can agree or disagree with any idea expressed in any work; it is their actions encouraged by such ideas that count. The books themselves are impotent. The phrases "the power of ideas" and "ideas have consequences" have meaning only in the context of action and in the volitional nature of men's minds. Ideas are not poison ivy.

The *Koran* can no more automatically influence a person to become a Muslim and/or a *jihadist* than *Atlas Shrugged* can automatically turn a reader into an intransigent champion of reason, individualism, and capitalism. The power of any fiction, nonfiction, religious, and scientific work, or of the ideas contained in them, depends on a reader's predisposition to any work's theme and purpose. If one is open to reason and rational answers, one will be influenced by *Atlas Shrugged*, and be impervious to or on guard against any appeal to the irrational. If one is open to mysticism, to the comfortably unknowable, envy, belonging to a group, an ethics that requires no thought, and to hatred of the good for being the good, one will be influenced by the *Koran*, and be immune to any appeal to reason.

If one composted copies of all the books mentioned in this commentary, and used the compost as fertilizer in one's garden, one's vegetables or flowers would not grow into inflammatory, poisonous, hate-inculcating monsters.

A *Koran*, when all is said and done, is merely a physical object, owned by someone, who is free to do with it what he wishes. He can burn it in protest of the ideas contained in it, or tear out its pages, or mulch it. Or he can read it, to better understand what he senses or has heard is objectionable and evil in it.

But treating what could be a personal misdemeanor or futile gesture, such as burning a book, as a capital crime is as much an act and instance of intolerance as an Islamic charge of blasphemy. Any law that protects the "feelings" or "dignity" of Muslims by incorporating "hate speech" laws into its legal system has taken the first crucial step to censorship and the subversion of secular law, including the negation of the First Amendment.

Burning a book is a concession to its author. It hands him a victory he would not have otherwise had.

February 2011

Circe in a Burqa

In Greek mythology, Circe was a beautiful sorceress who turned Odysseus' men into swine. With help from the god Hermes, Odysseus resisted Circe's charms, freed his men, and lived with her for a year. The story of Circe and Odysseus had a happy ending. Their union was passionate. Their parting was amicable.

In America, the Statue of Liberty is our Circe, holding aloft the torch of freedom for those who flee servitude and degradation to live their lives unimpeded by tyrants and mobs.

In Islam, Circe (or woman) is an innately corrupting creature, the equal of dogs and monkeys and monkeys, who must be covered from head to toe lest her charms lead Muslim men astray from the path of purity and righteousness and release the beast in them. It is a version of Christianity's original sin.

Sean Hannity recently had on his TV show two guests to discuss the recent ban in France of the burqa, and its proposed ban in Belgium: Bridgette Gabriel, president of the American Congress for Truth (ACT), and author of *They Must Be Stopped* and Edina Lekovic of the Muslim Public Affairs Council. It is a measure of the West's self-induced vulnerability, however, that all it can fear and combat are the outward manifestations of Islam. Such as the burqa.

The French ban of the burqa, and the proposed ban of it in Belgium, may be signs of an awakening but belated concern about the incremental Islamification of Europe. But the bans do not address the essential peril posed by Islam, which is its aggressive, all-consuming ideology. The banishers are unable or unwilling to attack that ideology. They forget or ignore the fact that the religion cannot be segregated from its politics; they are one and the same. There is probable truth to Gabriel's contention that where the burqa is worn in Western countries, that is where the "extremists" may be found. But will banning this degrading attire somehow alter the venues of alleged "extremism" or "radicalism"? No. Islam is by its nature radical and extremist, as radical, extremist, totalitarian, anti-reason, and anti-individual rights as was Nazism. One may as well have forbidden Nazis from wearing jackboots and flaunting the swastika. Islam is Islam.

Edina Lekovic for the MPAC claimed she is against the burqa, too, but insisted that it is a woman's choice to wear it. This is balderdash. It is worn because a woman is an obedient, brain-dead manquétte, or because she is forced to by order of some cleric's interpretation of the *Koran* and Hadith (there are four main schools of Islam), or from fear of reprisal from her husband, relatives and other Muslims if she does not wear it (that, or the chador, or a veil, or some clothing that neutralizes her feminine existence). In many Islamic countries, she would risk arrest by the religious police. No woman would consciously choose to wear the suffocating, gender-obliterating, self-existence-erasing garb. There is no rational reason for any woman to parade in public looking like an inhuman blob. In all instances of its being worn, it is evidence of mindless or fear-based submission. *Submission* is, after all, the *signature* act and virtue of Islam.

Towards the end of the Hannity segment, the host brought up the subject of Imam Faisal Rauf and the Ground Zero mosque. He ran a National Republican Trust ad against the Ground Zero mosque, which CBS and NBC refused to air. Gabriel had enough time to mention that Rauf's father was connected with the Muslim Brotherhood, the progenitor of all existing Islamic terror organizations, and that the mosque is an insult to those killed on 9/11. Lekovic claimed the mosque was inspired by an "exact opposite vision of Islam as the one that inspired the 9/11 hijackers," and more or less repeated Rauf's public statements about the mosque's purportedly benign purpose.

Hannity cited Rauf's statements in public and from Rauf's book, in an attempt to underscore the fact that what Islamists say in public, in English, to the West, is the exact opposite of what they really mean when addressing anyone in Arabic. Lekovic simply launched into her own panicky exhibit of *taqiya*, or the Islamic art of dissimulation, sanctioned by the *Koran.*

Allow me to quote briefly from Rauf's Wikipedia entry:

> In 1997, Abdul Rauf founded the American Society for Muslim Advancement, a civil society organization aimed at promoting positive engagement between American society and American Muslims. The organization is now headed by his wife, Daisy Khan. In 2003, Abdul Rauf founded the Cordoba Initiative, another registered nonprofit organization with offices in both New York and Kuala Lumpur, Malaysia. As CEO of Cordoba Initiative, Abdul Rauf coordinates projects that emphasize the bonds that connect the Muslim World and the West.

The name of his organization was carefully devised, but nevertheless is telltale. What exactly are Muslims "advancing" toward? Why do they need an organization to "advance" them? Do they not now enjoy the full benefits of citizenship? What else could there be an advancement to, unless it is a Sharia-compliant America? The acceptance of primitive, Dark Age Sharia law as a multiculturalist-tolerant "coequal" of Western, objective law? Yes. Rauf's organization is merely a smiley-face front for the conquest of America, just as CAIR and the MSA are. And Rauf himself has terrorist ties. These have been so thoroughly documented that it would be redundant to discuss them here.

What is equally telltale was Rauf's refusal to condemn Hamas, an organization that is inspired by the "exact opposite" of what purportedly inspires Rauf.

"Look, I'm not a politician. The issue of terrorism is a very complex question," he told WABC Interviewer Aaron Klein.

Asked again for his opinion on Hamas, an exasperated Rauf wouldn't budge. "I am a peace builder. I will not allow anybody to put me in a position where I am seen by any party in the world as an adversary or as an enemy," Rauf said, insisting that he wants to see peace in Israel between Jews and Arabs.

And, what bonds connect the Muslim World and the West? Are they the bonds of master and slave? No such bonds ever existed or exist now — unless we let them grow, and then they would become fetters. Hamas's conception of peace is the nonexistence of Israel. Rauf knows this.

The West and the Muslim World are not religious, but *ideological* antagonists.

Disagreement exists about the Ground Zero mosque. Some of it is honest disagreement. The preponderance of evidence that cites the mosque's actual purpose is on the side of those who oppose it. American liberty is under attack on at least two fronts: by our own government, and by Islam. Opposing the one attack to the neglect of the other still imperils us. Both attacks are of equal importance to me, posing the same mortal dangers, and both can be repelled and defeated by using the same arguments: if one opposes Islam (and Sharia law) because it violates individual rights, that is the same as opposing the government's violation of individual rights to impose de facto socialism. (The Islamists are also enemies of capitalism, and have made no bones about it.)

If we are addressing sentient beings whose minds are open to reason, they would concur with the corollary. If Sharia law is repugnant to American values for that reason, why should not secular socialism/fascism be equally repugnant? Switch the subjects around and ask the same question. The same argument can be made against Obamacare and similar legislation, such as financial reform, environmental regulations, and so on, as against all the totalitarian attributes of Islam.

The hypothetical victory of men of reason and advocates of individual rights that saw the retreat of statism might lay the groundwork for repelling the incursions of Islam. But, how long would it take to achieve such a victory? A generation or two? In the meantime, Islam would be "advancing" in this country. It is no coincidence that the left has allied itself with Islam and is friendly to any force that would vanquish its political institutions and Americans alike.

Defenders of the mosque backers' alleged property rights must concede that our situation is absurd and unprecedented: We are burdened with a government whose current stewards have a ravenous appetite for power, and who seem to not mind the incursions being made in this country by a rival ideology, because that incursion will also help to dissolve the country they hate and wish to "remake" as a "people's republic." Which one do we take up intellectual arms against first? This column has written with equal fervor about Obama and his policies as well, as it has against Islam and the Ground Zero mosque and the horrors of its own.

How, then, should one weigh the parallel evils? In both the short and long runs, which phenomenon poses the most immediate peril to American liberties? Should we suffer incremental impoverishment from socialism and fascism, or should we suffer the risk being maimed or murdered by a car bomb and have the American population at large become fair game for activist and intimidating domestic jihadists, as the Europeans are?

I can understand Leonard Peikoff's caveat during his recent podcast on the Ground Zero mosque, that his calm delivery should not be mistaken for disinterestness or distance from the subject. I do not think he ever imagined that the U.S. would descend to such an ignominious state and that the culture would become so irrational that it would defend its destroyers.

From my perspective, the insinuation by stealth and "tolerance" under the auspices of multiculturalism of Sharia law poses just as much a "clear and present danger" to me as the machinations of Obama, Pelosi, Reid, *et al.* to transform this country into one big prison of indentured servants to the state.

I reject with equal passion the prospect of Circe (or the Statue of Liberty) draped in a burqa, just as I reject the prospect of Barack Obama dressed as Uncle Sam.

July 2010

The Self-Defenseless West

Two oddly varying March 8th versions of the same commentary, "Caliphate, Jihad, Sharia: Now What?" by Raymond Ibrahim, associate director of the Middle East Forum, appear on the Middle East Forum (MEF) and the Hudson-New York sites. In both he begins by quoting a Columbia University professor from a 2008 debate, "Clash of Civilizations." The professor answered an "assertion that Islamists seek to resurrect the caliphate, and, according to the doctrine of offensive jihad, wage war – when and wherever expedient – to bring the world under Islamic rule."

> "Suppose you prove beyond any shadow of doubt that Islam is constitutionally [inherently] violent, where do you go from there?" (Brackets mine)

Ibrahim proceeds to describe a caliphate in two different ways. In the Hudson-New York version, he writes:

> A caliphate represents a permanent, ideological enemy, not a temporal enemy that can be bought or pacified through diplomacy or concessions — economic or otherwise.

In the MEF version, however, he writes:

> A jihad-waging, Sharia-enforcing caliphate represents a permanent, existentialist enemy—not a temporal foe that can be bought or pacified through diplomacy or concessions.

Note the difference. The term *ideological* is used as synonymous with *existentialist.* One might wonder why Ibrahim treats ideology as existential, except perhaps because it is a system of thought that exists and which has a measurable potency or influence. But ideologies, or ideas, do not exist independently of their progenitors, advocates, or exponents. Ideologies or ideas cannot act on their own; they must have "temporal" actors or men who carry them out. Islam is an "enemy" only in the person of jihadists who perform actions of both the physical and stealth kinds.

The jihad against the West is indeed temporal in nature, to either physically subjugate it, or destroy it.

Ibrahim then notes in the Hudson version what the establishment of a multinational caliphate would mean to the West.

The very existence of a caliphate would usher a state of constant hostility: Both historically and doctrinally, the caliphate is *obligated* to wage jihad, at least annually, to bring the "disbelieving" world under Islamic dominion and enforce Sharia law. Most of what is today called the "Muslim world"—from Morocco to Pakistan—was conquered, bit by bit, by a caliphate begun in Arabia in 632.

And in the MEF version:

Consider the caliphate: its very existence would usher in a state of constant hostility. Both historically and doctrinally, the caliphate's function is to wage jihad, whenever and wherever possible, to bring the infidel world under Islamic dominion and enforce Sharia. In fact, most of what is today called the "Muslim world"—from Morocco to Pakistan—was conquered, bit by bit, by a caliphate that began in Arabia in 632.

In truth, the West did face an enemy that waged constant warfare against it: the Soviet Union. So, there is a precedent for what the West now faces in the form of a totalitarian ideology albeit which Ibrahim later in the MEF version describes as one dressed in "religious garb." He speculates on what the West is or is not prepared to do about a caliphate. In his Hudson version, he asks:

Yet, as Western people begin to understand what is at stake, what exactly are their governments prepared to do about it — *now*, before the caliphate becomes a reality? Would the West be willing to launch a preemptive offensive — politically, legally, educationally, and, if necessary, militarily — if these were the only solutions to the establishment of a jihad-waging, Sharia-enforcing caliphate? Would it go on the offensive without waiting until its enemies were strong so that by the time one realized what was happening it would be too late, or would political correctness and pacifist inertia allow the Islamists to have their way?

And in the MEF version:

In this context, what, exactly, is the Western world prepared to do about it—*now*, before the caliphate becomes a reality? Would it be willing to launch a preemptive offensive—politically, legally, educationally, and, if necessary, militarily—to prevent its resurrection? Could the West ever go on the offensive, openly and confidently—*now*, when it has the upper-hand—to incapacitate its enemies?

It is noteworthy that Ibrahim substitutes *political correctness* and *pacifist inertia* with *openly* and *confidently* when he changes the thrust of his rhetorical question in the MEF version. It is also noteworthy that he leaves the *military* option until last. In the MEF version, he asserts that the West still has the "upper-hand." On the contrary, that hand is palsied. The West's "openness" and "confidence" have been disabled, if not completely amputated, by political correctness and pacifist inertia, not to mention by multiculturalism and unprincipled pragmatism of a succession of administrations.

And, openness and confidence about what? That the West is superior? That it is secular in nature, not religious? That the Mideast depends on its survival on the West? That there is no such thing as "Islamic" culture or an "Islamic civilization"? Was the Mafia crime empire, which stretched from Sicily to Chicago, with its warped code of ethics and use of force, fear, and murder, a "civilization"?

Ibrahim notes in the Hudson version:

The West, alarmingly, does not have a political history or language to justify an offensive against an ideological foe.

And in the MEF version:

The fact is, the West does not have the political paradigms or language to justify an offensive against an ideological foe in religious garb.

Actually, in the context of dealing with Islam, it does have such a "language" and a "political history" or "political paradigm," ranging from the Barbary Wars of the early 19th century to the battles of Omdurman and Umm Diwaykarat in 1898-99, in all instances acting with military force against Islamist depredations and expansionist designs, and with the knowledge, implicit or explicit, that Islam was inherently hostile to Western values and dedicated to removing them from human existence.

In the Hudson version, he notes:

Worse, as Arab governments come crashing down, the Obama administration has made it clear that it is willing to engage the Islamists and permit the Muslim Brotherhood to participate in elections, even before institutions of democracy — such as rule of law, an independent judiciary, and above all, free speech and a free press — have developed.

In the MEF version, he writes:

> Indeed, the Obama administration has already made it clear that it is
> willing to engage the Brotherhood, differentiating them from
> "radicals" like al-Quaeda—even as the Brotherhood's motto is "Allah
> is our objective, the prophet is our leader, the *Koran* is our law, jihad is
> our way, dying in the way of Allah our highest hope." Likewise, a
> theocratic, eschatologically-driven Iran is on its way to possessing
> nuclear weapons—all while the international community stands by.

It is unclear in Ibrahim's article whether he is underscoring his own
rhetorical question-begging and inability to provide answers, or the Columbia
professor's. But overall, Raymond Ibrahim's articles reveal a serious and fatal
indecision about what action should be taken against regimes that conduct
warfare against the West, and in particular against the U.S., with the aim of
subjugating it and imposing the Islamic ideology.

The West had the language and the resolve. And an important element
in that resolve was that no Western nation was a top-to-bottom welfare state,
was not "multicultural," did not deprecate or suborn the things its citizens
valued, such as individual rights, freedom from state interference in their
personal lives and actions, and the rule of objective law. The West in the 19th
century was riding on the mere momentum of an Aristotelian philosophy. But
the rise of welfare states and the inculcation of statism undercut and finally
arrested that momentum, and dissolved those things over decades of
philosophical and moral bankruptcy. The United States reached a point where
it elected a president who is actively anti-freedom, anti-reason, and
unabashedly pro-statist, willing to apologize to the world for the U.S.'s
greatness and working to see it diminished if not destroyed.

One could possibly date the phenomenon to WWI and the rise of
Progressivism early in the 20th century, and the steadfast implementation of
policies of pragmatism and appeasement. The roots of that phenomenon can be
traced clear back to the 18th and 19th centuries, when Immanuel Kant and his
successors launched an attack on Aristotelian thought, that is, on reason. The
West will remain helpless and impotent "in the face of an ideological foe
dressed in religious garb" unless it adopts an ideology that will identify that
foe and strip it of that garb for all to see.

That is not going to happen when our policymakers refuse to identify
Islam as the foe, but instead claim that Islam is fundamentally "peaceful" and
that it was "hijacked" by "extremists." One never heard FDR claim that
Nazism and Shintoism were "hijacked" by "extremists" or say that these
ideologies were somehow "radicalized." Even left-wing FDR had a quantum

of intellectual honesty that has put all of his successors to shame, including Eisenhower and Reagan.

It is the West's policies that have put it in the perilous position it is now in. I see no solution to the problem except a revolution in political thought and policy in this country. It is either that, or recognizing very quickly that only long-overdue retaliatory force will begin to solve the problem, such as eliminating states that sponsor terrorism before they eliminate us, of acknowledging that Islam is indeed an enemy in the persons of its subscribers. The same policy should apply to extinguishing Somali piracy, even at the risk of the lives of the captives of the pirates. Lancing that particular boil would be a good start.

Without an honesty and confidence founded on reason and rational values, and faced with the prospect of another "evil empire" in the form of a caliphate, the only direction the West can go is down to its own destruction. The confusion and hesitancy on the part of "experts" like Raymond Ibrahim are not encouraging.

March 2011

The Devilfish of Islamofascism

In *Toilers of the Sea*, one of Victor Hugo's lesser-known novels, is a marvelous description of how to defeat an enemy that is insidious by its nature, an enemy that has served as a symbol of the banal parasitism of evil. Towards the end of the novel, Gilliatt, the hero, is seized in an underwater cave by a devilfish, or octopus. The creature's tentacles cling to Gilliatt, and it is about to pierce his chest with its beak:

"The devilfish is cunning. It first tries to stupefy its prey. It seizes, then waits as long as it can.

"Gilliatt held his knife. The suction increased.

"All at once the creature detached its sixth tentacle from the rock, launched it at him, and attempted to seize his left arm....At the same time, it thrust its head forward swiftly....

"But Gilliatt was on his guard. Being watched, he watched.

"Gilliatt plunged the point of his knife into the flat, viscous mass, and with a twisting movement similar to the flourish of a whip, describing a circle around the two eyes, he tore out the head as one wrenches out a tooth.

"It was finished. The whole creature dropped.....The four hundred suckers simultaneously released their hold of the rock and the man.

"This rag sank to the bottom."

It is a passage our leaders ought to be made to read and learn from if they wish to successfully prosecute the "war against terrorism." The advocates and promulgators of Islamofascism, like the devilfish, stupefy their prey, and wait, then strike. Missing from the real life dilemma is a Gilliatt. President Bush is not one, nor is Prime Minister Tony Blair of Britain. They attack the tentacles but, in the name of tolerance, refuse to cut off the head.

As many contributors to this publication have pointed out, most recently and succinctly by Dr. Edwin Locke and Alex Epstein in their penetrating "The Terrorists' Motivation: Islam," the trouble is not that killers have "hijacked a peaceful religion." The trouble is that Islam is not, in its fundamental tenets (if its virulent injunctions can be called "principles"), a "peaceful" religion. It is a manifesto for the conquest and destruction of all Western civilization and the establishment of a global anti-man, anti0mind theocracy.

It pursues this goal, it should be apparent by now, by employing two methods: with immediate, violent action, such as indiscriminate bombings; and by an osmotic process of invading a Western country with a fifth column that works to alter Western laws to tolerate its presence, while at the same time preaching the abandonment of those laws in favor of law based on an intolerant *Koran*.

The *Koran* cannot be compromised, repudiated piecemeal, or "modified" so that it posed no threat to the West. It cannot be "secularized" without destroying Islam. Islam can no more be perverted or "hijacked" than can Nazism, Fascism, or Japanese Bushido. Islamic clerics know this, as well as rank-and-file Muslims, which is why they are largely silent on the matter of terrorism, with the exception of an occasional equivocating expression of public regret for the bombings.

The most serious problem is that the current conflict is being treated as a mere "war against terrorism." It has devolved into a mere cops0and-robbers manhunt for terrorists and suspected terrorists and their cells. It may as well be put on a par with a campaign to stamp out "violent bank robberies."

This is not to deprecate the heroic efforts of Britain's authorities in tracking down the London "Islamikazies" of 7/7, which includes a "shoot to kill" standing order and the suspension of the prohibition of "racial profiling" to identify suspects. But that is merely rounding up and obstructing the "foot soldiers" of the Islamofascists. The parties guilty of associating with the 7/7 bombers, and with the ones who botched a second round of London bombings and who are on the run, can be replaced, according to a British report, from among 16,000 militant British Muslims.

It would be interesting to know how many American Muslims are willing to don rucksacks and commit the same sabotage here. It is possible that such a report has been written and circulated among those agencies charged with identifying and "neutralizing" such "activists." But, for fear of offending American Muslims, very likely President Bush has forbidden its publication.

If we are at war with an insidious ideology, why limit our self-preservation actions to policing an invading army, while neglecting the goals and ends of its leaders?

The octopus head of Islamofascism is: Iran, Syria, and Saudi Arabia. To a lesser extent, one must include Pakistan and even Afghanistan, since the Taliban are apparently still active in both those countries and the heads of those countries are impotent or unwilling to eradicate them.

Most of the madrasses in Pakistan are subsidized by Saudi Arabia, and are a chief source of suicide bombers. One might argue that Iraq was a good starting place to eradicate our enemy. But why the U.S. should be expending lives and fortune to establish a "democratic" government there, beggars explanation and reason. After Saddam Hussein and his government had been overthrown, we should have moved on to Syria or Iran and let the Iraqis sort out what to do next. We are under no moral obligation to help anyone discover the benefits of Western institutions, not at the price of sacrificing American lives, American wealth, and American liberties, which is what is occurring now.

Our leaders must recognize that the head must be lopped off before any substantive progress can be made against alien or resident terrorists. Until they learn that lesson, the bombings and killings and mayhem will continue unabated. The devilfish has watched, waited, and struck repeatedly ever since the World Trade Center bombing since 1993. It has taken the measure of our resolve and of our ignorance. It is neither shocked nor awed.

Now, a very strange thing happened when Admiral Karl Donitz arranged the German surrender to the Allies in 1945: the European war was over.

Another strange thing happened when General Douglas MacArthur received the Japanese surrender on the battleship Missouri in 1945: the Pacific war was ended.

And a third strange thing occurred when World War Two was declared over and became history: the Allies ceased worrying that the war would continue within the borders of their own countries.

The heads were lopped off, the tentacles died when the primitive brain that guided them was gone, and the rags of Nazism and Bushido sank to the bottom.

Whatever fifth columnists and sympathizers existed in the U.S. and Britain did not carry on the fight for Nazism or the Emperor after German and Japanese governments surrendered and were reconstituted. Many Nazis fled justice to South America, to Egypt, to other safe havens. And the Allies did not wring their hands over "human rights" and trials until after the war, in Nuremberg. Then it was the rights of the millions of murdered that concerned the judges, not the rights of the accused members of the governments guilty of those crimes.

The same thing would happen to Islam, if the West had enough self-esteem and resolve to fight the war as it should be fought: by taking the war to the enemy. Islam would scurry back into its self-made Dark Age and pose no threat to those who wished to live without vengeful mullahs and imams looking over their shoulders. Muslims who chose to remain in the West would need to learn to submit to Western laws of individual rights and the separation of church and state. If they do not choose to submit to those laws, they should be invited to emigrate to those nations whose ethics and society are more fitting to their refusal to think.

Whatever Islamic terrorist cells might exist in the U.S., Britain, France and other Western nations, would wither away for lack of funding, guidance and even purpose. They would not and could not "carry on the fight."

Where would the West be today if Churchill and Roosevelt were stupefied and adopted the Bush/Blair philosophy of fighting an enemy intent on conquest? Where would we be if they had restricted their combat operations to fighting saboteurs, provocateurs, and secret agents on the "home front"?

Where would we be if they had not judged Nazism and Bushido as inimical to Western civilization?

Would we have won World War Two if we had "tolerated" Nazism and Japanese imperialism as multiculturalist "peers" of our own political system, and merely sought to prevent their saboteurs from bombing schools and subways? Would we have won if we regarded Nazism as just another "belief system" that had been "hijacked" by Hitler?

Where would the West be today if Churchill and Roosevelt had adopted the Bush/Blair method of confronting our enemies?

I am certain of this: I would not be asking these questions. I might not be. I might have been liquidated for refusing to bow to the Emperor or to shout "Sieg heil!"

And I have ample proof of my possible fate should I refuse to bow to Mecca. That is why I will not discard my knife of reason and my love of existence.

July 2005

Everybody Drew a Fatwa

The Islamists mean to censor us one way or another: if not from fear of retaliation, then by retaliation. Shut your mouth, still your pens, stop thinking, or we will do it for you. Permanently.

Molly Norris, mild-mannered cartoonist, started a fire she cannot put out. As Rick Santelli's "rant" on TV from the floor of the Chicago Board of Trade fueled the Tea Party, Norris inspired thousands revolt against Islam. In a desiderative whim, she drew innocuous, refrigerator-door magnet caliber pictures which she claimed were images of Mohammad: a spool of thread, a teacup, a spoon, and other mundane things. Overall, they looked more like idle doodles than passionate expressions of the freedom of speech. She posted them in protest of Viacom's Comedy Central forbidding its cartoon show, "South Park," to depict Mohammad in a bear suit.

That spawned the immensely popular "Everybody Draw Mohammed Day!" on Facebook. And thousands did draw. It is interesting to note that one can invite people to "draw Lincoln," and we would see images of Lincoln ranging from good to unrecognizable. But how does one draw an image of a person whose face has never been seen, except in imagination? Imagination took hold.

Numerous responses have appeared on Facebook where artists comment, "We have reached 50,000 members. As the news of the rebellion against the attacks to our liberties is heard, brave people join the campaign to stave of those who would annihilate that which we believe in, freedom. Thomas Jefferson's quote is also on the Facebook page. "All tyranny needs to gain a foothold is for people of good conscience to remain silent."

Americans and their friends across the globe responded en masse. The defiance was overwhelming, producing more cartoons than the Danish could draw, many of them ingenious. For a while, everyone was a Guy Fawkes, or a Paul Revere, or a Joan of Arc.

But — Molly Norris was criticized. Islam answered. Muslims demonstrated. Shut up. Molly Norris recanted. She didn't mean to offend Muslims. She was only expressing her right to freedom of speech. Facebook also caved to Muslim demands and took down the page.

Too late. Contrition doesn't carry much weight in Islam. No one has a right to offend Islam, or blaspheme against it. Whether Mohammad is depicted as a pedophilic ogre, as a knock-off of Charlton Heston's Moses, or as a teacup, it matters not. It is forbidden. "Sorry" doesn't cut it.

A fatwa has been issued against her and anyone who participated in Everybody Draw Mohammad Day. It appeared in an Al Qaeda online "magazine" and was issued by a former American turned Muslim cleric, Anwar Al-Awlaki, who now lives in hiding in Yemen. Molly Norris is now a "prime target" to be murdered.

"A cartoonist out of Seattle, Washington, named Molly Norris started the 'Everyone Draw Mohammed Day,'" the article attributed to the radical Yemeni cleric says. "She should be taken as a prime target of assassination, along with others who participated in her campaign."The large number of participants makes it easier for us because there are many targets to choose from," reads the article in the magazine of Al-Qaeda in the Arabian Peninsula, or AQAP.

The killings should not, however, be limited to "Draw Mohammed" participants, the article says. "Because (participants) are practicing a 'right' that is defended by the law, they have the backing of the entire Western political system. This would make... attacking any Western target legal from an Islamic viewpoint."

Molly Norris should know that Islamic "legality" is consistently irrational and brutal. It is not a matter of a slap on the wrist and a fine. Submission to Islam must be total — or not at all. The "justice" meted out to those who only partially submit is perilous. Even Muslims are not exempt from it.

So, Molly Norris's life, and that of anyone who drew Mohammad on Facebook, is in danger. So is the right to freedom of speech. The law that defends it is also fair game. The First Amendment is targeted for assassination, as well, not only by President Barack Obama's wannabe censors, but by Islamists who want to replace the Constitution with Sharia law. Anwar All-Whacky is just as determined to see censorship imposed as is Cass Sunstein (by government force) or Stanley Fish (censorship by proxy). Excuse the mocking nickname; my powers of illustration fail me.

Stanley Fish, self-appointed academic ombudsman of free speech, quibbles about the use of the term *censorship*, not understanding, or not wishing to understand, that if fear results in the silencing of speech — a fear sired by the threat of direct force, or of a costly, ruinous lawsuit — that is as much censorship as the employment of force itself.

So what Random House did was not censorship. (Some other press is perfectly free to publish Jones's book, and one probably will.) It may have been cowardly or alarmist, or it may have been good business, or it may have been an attempt to avoid trouble that ended up buying trouble. But whatever it was, it doesn't rise to the level of constitutional or philosophical concern. And it is certainly not an episode in some "showdown between Islam and the Western tradition of free speech." Formulations like that at once inflate a minor business decision and trivialize something too important and complex to be reduced to a high-school civics lesson about the glories of the First Amendment.

Fish manages to denigrate not only Salman Rushdie in his New York Times piece, but also business itself. He has no grasp of what is fundamentally of "constitutional or philosophical concern." It's all so trivial, nothing to get worked up about. Save your concern for something important. And that would be...?

"The large number of participants makes it easier for us because there are many targets to choose from," boasted All-Whacky. True. How are he and his American proxies going to find and slay 50,000 offenders? No problem. He has designated any Western target for destruction. Perhaps someone who "drew Mohammad" will be one of the bomb victims.

How better to vitiate the First Amendment than to frighten men from upholding it? Those who refrain from drawing Mohammad, or from satirizing him and his Moonie-like flocks in word or deed out of "respect" or "tolerance," or from sheer funk, or who counsel others to refrain, are just as culpable in the loss of that liberty as any Washington censor or duty-bound Muslim.

Of course, one needn't have drawn Mohammad to become a prime target for assassination. Watching a soccer match in Uganda is also a punishable offense. Or publishing an Islam-friendly novel about the adventures of Mohammad's child bride — without illustrations. Or an imageless history of the images of Mohammad. Or employing terms that identify the enemy in national security reports (that would be "profiling" a "religion of peace").

Those who drew Mohammad last spring cannot all go into hiding, as doubtless Molly Norris must now do. The FBI has advised her to take the threat seriously. There are countless Muslims — itinerate loners or residents of Muslim enclaves in this country or the patrons of the proposed Ground Zero Mosque — willing to do All-Whacky's bidding. We are at war with Islam, and the enemy is amongst us.

Is America fated to become a nation-in-hiding? You, the reader, decide. Our government will not acknowledge the war declared against us. It is up to Americans acknowledge it, and to never surrender this country to Islam or to its secular, Obama-esque form — to never let it go.

July 2010

Rednecks and Hijabs

A very apt analogy occurred to me as I read some news items about how certain individuals and groups wish to lasso the First Amendment and put it in a corral. For those who doubt that censorship is creeping ever closer, or are confused about the various issues and see no connections between them at all, the analogy will help to concretize the phenomenon.

We have all heard the joke with a thousand variations, such as, "You're a redneck if your front yard boasts three rusty washing machines and seven cars sitting on cinder blocks." Does a rank-and-file Muslim differ much from the legendary American redneck? Fundamentally, no. What defining characteristics do they share? They are notoriously non-intellectual, mentally arrested, tribal in outlook, and prefer to stick to traditional ways of living and of doing things. On the latter characteristic, they are hostile to the prospect of venturing into new and possibly better ways of thinking, living and doing things, and resent the imposition of having to think and choose. They prefer to be left alone to exist in an insular universe of the mundane and the perceptually familiar.

Their reading habits are mainly limited to violent and bloody ghost stories, that is, to the Bible and the *Koran*, which represent the limits of their grasp of a moral code. What they do not share are a thirst for alcohol and their traditional cuisines. A Muslim would faint with horror or walk away in a holy snit if served a plate of chitterlings by a waitress in a Hooters outfit, while the redneck would feel offended if offered Southern-fried goat meat or a falafel fajita. But they are otherwise cognitively inert, passive manqués who unthinkingly heed the advice of their Bible- and *Koran*-thumping spiritual leaders.

Their more "advanced" or ambitious brethren are activists of many suasions. For the redneck, these are represented by the Ku Klux Klan and religious conservative politicians. For the Muslim, these are represented by Hezbollah, Hamas, Al-Qaeda and the Council on American-Islamic Relations or any of its well-heeled "watchdog" clone organizations throughout the country. The "activists" believe that the status quo, tradition and God's writ can be preserved for all time with violence or by insinuating their oppressive creeds into the larger polity under the sly guises of "tolerance" and "moral uplift and purity."

To this end, the Klan believed in instilling terror and obedience in the minds of Negroes, Jews, and Catholics, and in staging house burnings or lynchings to prove they meant business. Hezbollah, Hamas, and Al-Qaeda believe in instilling wholesale terror in the minds of any group they designate "unbelievers" and blowing up as many of them as possible, and in a dozen or so beheadings and dismemberments, to show that they mean business.

The Klan would leave alone those who "knew their place" and submitted humbly to its "superior" moral code and a Jim Crow political system. Islamic activists claim they will leave alone those who humbly accept the status of dhimmitude and acknowledge their subjugation to a "superior" moral code and a theocratic leviathan, also known as a caliphate. The Jim Crow enforcers would impose a poll tax on those who were barred from voting and all participation in politics. The Islamists would impose a jizya on non-Muslims, and that would be the limit of theocratic politics in the caliphate, for Muslim and redneck unbeliever alike.

Enough of the analogy. I think the point is made. Two of the news items that triggered this diversion are these:

On December 13th, in "Our Saudi Foes" (in this anthology) I remarked on how CAIR received, at CAIR's instigation, submission from the Fox network and diluted the moral appeal of "24" by "humanizing" Jack Bauer's Islamic enemies or by simply diversifying his enemies so that they weren't always Muslims. British Muslims, however, are bolder and are going after bigger game.

Lawrence Van Gelder, in a New York Times article on January 26th, reported in "Arts, Briefly," that:

"A British Islamic group complained yesterday that Western films as old as 'Raiders of the Lost Ark' in 1981 have promoted a negative stereotype of Muslims, Reuters reported. The group's report called upon British censors to be given expanded power to cut 'objectionable material' and urged cultural watchdogs to be more effective in ensuring 'responsible coverage' of Muslims. 'There is no such thing as a Muslim good guy,' complained Arzu Merali, a coauthor of the report by the Islamic Human Rights Commission. Its study, attributed to responses from nearly 1,200 British Muslims, said that 62 percent felt the British media were 'Islamophobic,' and 14 percent called them racist. 'Cinema, both in Hollywood and Britain, has helped to demonize Muslims,' Mr. Merali said. 'They are portrayed as violent and backward. That reinforces prejudices.'"

As "violent and backward" as rednecks? Do not for a moment think that Mr. Merali and his colleagues on the Commission are unaware that it is Muslims who are raising holy hell – otherwise known as jihad – all around the world in a kind of global Hatfield and McCoy feud against each other's sects and everyone else, if the daily death toll in Baghdad is any measure. They are hoping that the employment of the term "prejudice" will scare off anyone who might make that point and ask that a Muslim "good guy" to be pointed out to him. They are hoping that no one remembers that uncounted thousands of

Muslims around the world cheered the destruction of the World Trade Center on 9/11 and the Madrid and London and Bali bombings, as well, and hailed the perpetrators as "good guys," if not heroes.

Indiana Jones or James Bond impersonators they were not. By *Koranic* standards, can there be such a thing as a Muslim "good guy"? The only Muslim "good guys" one can observe are the so-called "moderates" who express queasiness about the actions their "extremist" champions take against especially Westerners, but who won't lift a finger in protest against such "stereotyping."

"Prejudice"? A year ago I stopped patronizing a Muslim-owned tobacco shop for two reasons: I couldn't be sure that some of its revenue was being extorted by or "donated" Mafia-style to Islamic organizations up in northern Virginia's "Jihad Alley" that in turn funneled the money to terrorist gangs with *sub rosa* connections to CAIR and other domestic Islamic entities; and because I grew tired of seeing the otherwise gorgeous Muslim woman at the register going to fat and seed, garbed in hijab, and deferring humbly to her scruffy-looking Muslim husband. Call me prejudiced. I can live with the disapprobation.

Mr. Merali should not worry about Hollywood ever offending Muslim sensibilities or stereotyping Muslims. Other than producing a few insipid films that dealt with 9/11 but which barely mentioned or didn't mention Muslims at all, Hollywood has been resoundingly silent on the subject of Islamic jihad. In fact, the one portrayal of a Muslim that should not offend Muslims is that of Naveen Andrews, who plays the competent and eminently rational Sayid on ABC's "Lost." As a former Iraqi Republican Guard, Sayid has only once taken time to bow to Mecca. (I watch the program because I like some of the characters in it, but I have no idea where it is headed, and I don't think its producers and director knew where it was going, either, when they premiered it.)

Let us turn to the redneck notion of imposing dhimmitude. The Wilmington, North Carolina Star on January 26th carried a story, "Republican: Scripts need reviewing, Movie prompts lawmaker's incentive idea."

> "Citing the controversy surrounding the Dakota Fanning film 'Hounddog,' the leader of the state Senate [Phil Berger] says he wants the government to review scripts before cameras start rolling in North Carolina.

> "That system, said Berger, would apply only to films seeking the state's lucrative filmmaker incentive, which refunds as much as 15 percent of what productions spend in North Carolina from the state treasury. 'Why should North Carolina taxpayers pay for something

they find objectionable?' said Berger, who is having proposed legislation drafted."

In the film, 12-year-old Dakota Fanning's character reportedly is subjected to a graphically filmed rape. Berger may find the scene "objectionable," and so may many of his redneckier Christian constituents.

But, why indeed are North Carolina taxpayers being forced to subsidize filmmakers? In addition to the Corporation for Public Broadcasting, and the National Endowment for the Arts, and the National Endowment for the Humanities? And any other governmental, tax-financed program that promotes "culture," whether or not it produces anything deemed of any esthetic merit? The artistic value or content, or lack of it, of a film is irrelevant. The article goes on to explain Berger's "objections":

> "State law denies the incentive to films that are obscene. In state law, obscenity is defined as depicting sexual conduct presented in an offensive way that appeals to prurient interest, lacks any 'serious literary, artistic, political or scientific value,' and is not free speech protected by the state or federal constitutions."

And who typically has the power to determine "serious literary, artistic, political or scientific" values? An appointed bureaucrat, otherwise known as a censor.

> "Berger said the film-incentive ban should be broadened to include material considered objectionable. He said there should be no First Amendment concerns because the producer would be seeking money from the state government. But he did say that if constitutional questions confused the matter, it would be better not to have a film incentive at all."

True enough, and if the film incentive program were ever dropped, it would save Berger the bother and embarrassment of pondering the true meaning of the First Amendment. But nascent censors like Berger usually think of something else to spend taxpayer money on. Constitutional matters will always confuse or confound his ilk, but won't stop them from taking advantage of the confusion. It should be pointed out, however, that censoring films subsidized by the government is only one step away from censoring films not subsidized by it, on the grounds that they contain "objectionable" material or have no "definable" social or artistic value.

For a clue to what else other than badly made movies may be deemed "objectionable," please refer back to my commentary on the British Muslims above. What the Muslims and rednecks have in mind to fit over everyone's minds is not anything as skimpy as a veil or a hijab. It is a burka.

February 2007

Islamic Ambulance Chasers

I wrote an open letter of protest to U.S. District Court, Chief Judge Vicki Miles-LaGrange, Oklahoma City, in response to the news that she had blocked an amendment to Oklahoma's constitution that would prohibit state and local judges from factoring Sharia and international law into their decisions.

The Associated Press reported:

A federal judge issued a temporary restraining order Monday to block a new amendment to the Oklahoma Constitution that would prohibit state courts from considering international or Islamic law when deciding cases.

Why? Is not the judge sworn to uphold the U.S. Constitution, as well as that of the state of Oklahoma? Well, she doesn't think so, and neither does Muneer Awad. *Who?*

"My constitutional rights are being violated through the condemnation of my faith," said Muneer Awad, executive director of the Council on American-Islamic Relations in Oklahoma. "Islam was the target of this amendment. This amendment does not have a secular purpose."

Wrong. It does have a secular purpose: to stop Islamic religious Sharia law from insinuating itself into American secular law. And wouldn't you know it? A bill for amendment was introduced into the Oklahoma state legislature, passed, and approved by the voting electorate by 70%. Whether you call that "democracy at work," or the proper procedure of a rights-protecting republic, the shills for Sharia object very much to self-governance. The Council on American-Islamic Relations (CAIR) jumped on it immediately, waving the unsheathed sword of lawsuits.

During a radio interview on WABC on November 7th, Awad, who graduated from law school, claimed that:

… Shariah is compliant with both American values and its Constitution, since the Islamic law is "dynamic" in that it changes based on circumstances, including governing law of lands where implemented.

There's a serving of *Taqiyya* Supreme for you. Sharia is not "compliant" with American values and the Constitution. The Constitution was designed to protect individual rights; Sharia does not recognize individual rights, neither its religious nor its political side. In any event, the *Koran* regards all other man-made governments as "abominations" to be eliminated.

And I wonder how Mr. Awad can reconcile his statement with that of Omar M. Ahmad, chairman of the board of CAIR, who said to Muslims in 1998:

> "If you choose to live here (in America) . . . you have a responsibility to deliver the message of Islam," he said. "Islam isn't in America to be equal to any other faith, but to become dominant," he said. "The *Koran*, the Muslim book of scripture, should be the highest authority in America, and Islam the only accepted religion on Earth."

Awad, among other claims, asserts that the law "stigmatizes" Muslims. *Wrong.* The fact that the overwhelming majority of terrorist attacks in this country and around the world, are committed by Muslims in the name of Islam, stigmatizes them. And the primitive, brutal, Dark Age legal and moral code that comprises Sharia law stigmatizes Sharia, as well.

Why was this amendment passed by the state legislature and put up for referendum?

The measure's author, Rep. Rex Duncan, R-Sand Springs, attended the brief court hearing and said afterward he was surprised by Miles-Lagrange's decision.

> "It thwarts the will of the people," said Duncan, an attorney who was elected district attorney in the northern Oklahoma counties of Osage and Pawnee in the general election.

> Duncan has said the constitutional amendment was not intended as an attack on Muslims but an effort to prevent activist judges from relying on international law or Islamic law when ruling on legal cases.

> That is an eminently clear reason for approving the amendment. But, "activist" judges? Is Judge LaGrange an "activist" judge? Has Duncan any grounds for making that *stigmatizing* allegation?

It turns out that Vicki Miles-LaGrange, a former state senator, was appointed in 1994 to the federal bench in Oklahoma, Western District, by President Bill Clinton, and has sat as chief judge there since 2008. It is interesting, also, that among the 367 judges nominated by him and still active in the federal system during his administration, he also elevated Sonia Sotomayor to the U.S. Court of Appeals for the Second Circuit in 2008. She was subsequently nominated and elevated to the Supreme Court by President Barack Obama. Another "activist," former Harvard Law School dean and

Solicitor General Elena Kagan, since elevated to the high court, is Obama's own creature. Would liberal/left/collectivist presidents nominate any judge to a high court whose political affinities and agendas did not mesh with their own?

My letter follows:

9 November 2010

Vicki Miles-LaGrange, Chief Judge
U.S. Courthouse
200 N.W. Fourth St.
Room 3301 (Third Floor)
Oklahoma City, OK 73102

Courtroom 301 (Third Floor)
Chambers Telephone: 405-609-5400
Chambers Fax: 405-609-5413

Dear Judge LaGrange:

> *Re your very recent decision to suspend voter certification of the referendum to bar the introduction of Sharia law into American jurisprudence.*
> *Here are some perorations for you, from a major Horse's Mouth, about Sharia law:*

> *"Those who know nothing about Islam pretend that Islam counsels against war. Those people are witless. Islam says: 'Kill all the unbelievers just as they would kill you all!' Does this mean that Muslims should sit back until they are devoured by the infidel? Islam says: 'Kill them, put them to the sword and scatter them.'*

> *"Islam says: 'Whatever good there is exists thanks to the sword.' The sword is the key to Paradise, which can be opened only for the Holy Warriors! Does all this mean that Islam is a religion that prevents men from waging war? I spit upon those foolish souls who make such a claim."*

> *The Horse? Ayatollah Ruhollah Khomeini. But, don't take his word for it. Consult the Koran.*
> *Sharia law would forbid you, a female, from being a judge, or having any kind of education or career goal beyond knitting, cooking, and child-bearing. Sharia would insist that you wear a burqa or niqab, or some other garb in public that would hide and denigrate your sex. Sharia would permit your husband to beat you and otherwise abuse you in all sorts of inhuman ways, and*

you would have no recourse to objective, rights-protecting law, because his actions would be motivated by the beast's "religious beliefs." Sharia would, if your eye ever roamed and fixed upon another man, permit the "community" to stone you to death. The advocates of Sharia wish to first, insinuate Sharia law into American jurisprudence, as they have in British law, then pursue the main goal of supplanting it with Sharia. Founders and current executives of CAIR, Mr. Awad's mother organization, have said so repeatedly in public.

Your "honor"? Forgive me for neglecting to mention the "honor" killings of women and girls for straying from Islamic ways. "Your honor" would take on a completely different meaning, no? All this and much more would be permitted in your own country.

This is what you're sanctioning by blocking the Oklahoma law. Or are you a bean-counting judge, able to see concrete things, but not the total picture? Are you an anti-conceptual mentality, unable to project consequences from causes? Either way, you have demonstrated by this act that you are as much a danger to America as any suicide bomber, and ought to be disqualified or cited by the American Bar Association, if there is any reason left in that organization.

This advisory has been sent as an open letter to leading Oklahoma newspapers.

Regards.....

November 2010

Islam the Alien

For me, most science fiction stories have a credibility problem. But the one branch of it whose premise I have always rejected is that alien life could be both malevolent and technologically advanced enough to embark on interstellar conquests. Films such as *Predator* and *Independence Day* – just two of the more popular instances of the genre among many – portray aliens stalking man as a species of game or subjugating or extinguishing him. The premise that projects the possibility of these creatures is that a preeminently hostile, anti-life-form could somehow apply reason to create spaceships and sophisticated weaponry.

However, life-forms so malevolent would never rise from the rank swamps that bred them to go zipping around star systems and blasting planets to atoms. Malevolence is not a progenitor of innovation or creation. It is fundamentally a parasite and can thrive only on a passive or willing host. Reason is not an attribute or a handmaiden of evil. Evil in fact can only exploit the products of reason, but never originate them. Evil men or evil aliens may exhibit *intelligence*, but not reason. They can exploit what reason has caused to exist, but never bring it into existence

Ugly predators and slimy aliens that can invent cloaking devices and disintegrating rays are possible in imagination only because of a fantastic, and possibly even fatal, fallacy. Their creators – and their fans – assume that reason is not the natural antithesis and enemy of anti-reason, but a morally neutral faculty that can ally itself with anti-reason in campaigns of conquest and death.

Not so coincidentally, the fallacy also explains the left's hostility to freedom and capitalism. Capitalists, they say, have the freedom to employ reason to create things, and then use their profits to establish power and enslave everyone.

Sharks, rattlesnakes, Komodo dragons, wolves, and other predators are not inherently evil. They do what nature has programmed them to do, without any choice in their struggles for existence. No moral decisions are involved in their actions. Their values are predetermined. They lack the attribute of volition, that is, the capacity to think or not to think, to choose what will sustain and improve their lives and what will not.

A malevolent intelligence is not a contraction in terms. Else how to explain all the real and fictional villains in history and literature, from Hitler to Professor Moriarty, from Attila the Hun to Ellsworth Toohey? Or Iran's Mahmoud Ahmadinejad and his threatened nuclear weapons? But a malevolent adherent to reason, like the aliens in *Predator* and *Independence Day*, is a psychological, metaphysical and philosophical contradiction. In nature, the teleology of such alien creatures is impossible.

A malevolent intelligence may succeed in finding comfort in a social and material environment created by reason, and be able to exploit its victims' innocence, foolishness, or ignorance. But without reason having created such a world, it would remain a miserable prisoner in the dank, fetid jungle it was born in, never able to conceive of anything better, unable by its nature to look up at the stars, content with its surroundings, and concerned only with its next meal. Thomas Hobbes' notion of man at war is equally and more realistically applicable to the actual existence of would-be predator space aliens in their basic mode: solitary, poor, nasty, brutish, and short.

Which leads me to Islam.

Islam is a malevolent, ideational predator bent on conquest. It demands conversion, submission, or death. Left to its own devices, Islam would have remained contained by and confined to its own impotence whence it came, the Mideast, in Saudi Arabia. It would be a bubonic rat that squeaked but which would otherwise be quarantined by its own irrationality, and by reason.

But what has given Islam its purported potency to wreck havoc in the world? It is a philosophy burdened with the same fallacy that allows science fiction writers to believe that reason can ally with anti-reason and act of its own accord. In past columns I have likened Islam to a drooling beast, to the Borg, to a viral disease, and to other entities closed to reason, proof against freedom, and dedicated to destruction for destruction's sake.

Pragmatic policies in the West allowed the nomadic, primitive Saudis and other tribalists to nationalize the oil which Western technology discovered and developed in the barren wastes over which they had been butchering each other and other tribes for millennia. Environmentalist policies that prohibit oil drilling allow smug tribalists to make extortion a practical policy. Pragmatic policies allowed Muslims to immigrate to semi-free, semi-rational cultures and proceed to complete the sabotaging disease of irrationality. Pragmatism sired moral and cultural relativism that forbids moral judgment of Islam's barbarism and its incipient, cradle-to-grave psychosis. Appropriating the mantle of "religious freedom" – call it a "cloaking device," if you will – and exploiting the foolishness and irrationality of their enemies, Islamic activists in three-piece suits and armed with unlimited funds work obsessively to erase freedom for all but Muslims.

Pragmatism fosters the growth of a police state whose managers and minions, in the name of political correctness and non-discrimination, will not identify Islam as a predatory ideology (that would be evidence of "Islamophobia," and "offensive"), and proceed to subject and inure a country's citizens to the invasive ministrations of arbitrary searches, seizures, and incarceration on the chance that they might catch a bomber whose motives will not be linked to Islam. Their policy, designed to not offend Muslims but all non-Muslims, is to hope to find a scimitar in an infinite haystack. The

Department of Homeland Security is headed by a multiculturalist friendly to Islam, while the TSA is staffed by tens of thousands of non-entities empowered to grope, violate, molest, rob, and hold judgment over private citizens in the name of "safety."

The anti-profiling policies of the DHS and TSA are anti-reason, and anti-Aristotelian, and as "alien" as the ends of a Predator or shapeless alien piloting five-mile-wide spaceships.

Islam is such a unique, unprecedented peril that one ignores it at one's own peril. There is the double peril of Obama, Pelosi, et al. (and the generations of collectivist thought behind them) wanting to "transform" the country into a secular State of Servitude (no pun intended), and of Islam, whose spokesmen are at work insinuating its brand of totalitarianism into the country via "religious freedom," but whose purpose is also to "transform" the country into another kind of State of Servitude. In this teleological end Islamists have a willing ally, the secular totalitarians.

Saul Alinsky, meet Sheikh Ahmad Gad of the Muslim Brotherhood, another malevolent intelligence.

Islam is a radically different matter. None of the other religious groups in America – whether they are composed largely of immigrants or of tenth generation blacks or whites or Asians or Eskimos — expects the other creeds to defer to it. Muslims and Islam, however, expect everyone to defer to Islam. Islam is an enemy of individualism. Islam is imbued with a code of conduct that is fundamentally barbaric and concrete-bound and too often murderous. Sharia is not just a primitive system of adjudication; it is also, and inherently, political. It does not recognize the world beyond that insular system, except as something to assimilate into its system, or to erase.

The corrupting norms of multiculturalism have vastly aided Muslims in their not having to knuckle under secular law and having to stop murdering wayward daughters and wives and sons who become apostates. Furthermore, feminists, liberals, leftists in and out of academia ignore the outrages committed by Muslims in the name of Islam – the continuing rapes of 'infidel" women in Europe and the Mideast by Muslims, the stonings, hangings, and executions of men and women who flout Islamic rules, the persecution and murders of Christians, Jews, Hindus in the name of Islam, and so on – because they recognize Islam as a bird of the same feather – a totalitarian system that shares similar premises, methods, and ends. Criticism of rival totalitarians might inadvertently lead to criticism of their own anti-reason and anti-life policies. Call the phenomenon a Collectivist-Islamic Non-Aggression Pact.

Predatory "aliens" need not come from outer space. There are two species of them right here on earth, both exercising their malevolent intelligences to advance their dual agendas of conquest, slavery, and destruction. They are merely rivals, and not antipodes of each other.

As Gilliatt did in Victor Hugo's compelling novel, *Toilers of the Sea*, as he was being enveloped by an octopus's arms, and as the creature's flesh-tearing beak struggled to strike him, we need to free ourselves from Islamic jihad not by cutting off its arms: but its head. Only reason and rationality can accomplish that end. That done, the arms will go limp and release us to pursue our life-affirming values in freedom without peril or hindrance. It is the ideology that must be damned, renounced, repudiated, and defeated, with no apologies or regrets, and not its surface manifestations.

Then we will have the time to turn our attention to performing the same surgery on the secular totalitarian ideology that also seeks to vanquish this country.

July 2011

The Battle of Tours, by Charles de Steuben, 1837

Mohammadan Enterprises

The New Pyramid Builders

A mile-high tower will rise in a desert port town, and Americans will be helping to finance its £5 billion construction cost. It will rise in the town Jeddah, Saudi Arabia, halfway up the length of the Red Sea.

At 5,250 feet, it will be twice the height of another tower being erected in Dubai, United Arab Emirates, on the Persian Gulf. A few miles north up the Sea from Jeddah is Rabigh, where about 40,000 workers are constructing the world's largest petrochemical plant as part of King Abdullah Economic City, itself part of a $500 billion plan to turn Saudi Arabia into a "powerhouse" industrial giant. Other massive construction projects are underway in Kuwait and other Persian Gulf countries.

"By the end of the year," reported *The New York Times* in an article, "The Construction Site Called Saudi Arabia," on January 20,

"This massive city of steel at the edge of the Red Sea will take its place as a cog of globalization: plastics produced here will be used to make televisions in Japan, cell phones in China and thousands of other products to be sold in the United States and Europe. Construction costs at the plant, which spreads over eight square miles, have doubled to $10 billion because of shortages in materials and labor. The amount of steel being used is 10 times the weight of the Eiffel Tower."

The *Times* article also reports that,

"Abu Dhabi is planning to spend close to $1 billion for a new museum with the help of the Louvre, in Paris. Dubai's latest grandiose idea is to build a small-scale replica of the French city of Lyon, complete with residential housing, a museum, a culinary school and a soccer club."

Americans will be helping to finance these and other massive projects in Saudi Arabia and in the Persian Gulf fiefdoms through their gas and heating oil prices. One important thing to remember about these projects is that they are not strictly "private" undertakings; every one of them is a government project. Strictly speaking, neither Saudi Arabia nor any of the other medieval kingdoms or satrapies in the Mideast has a "government," representative or otherwise.

Their legislative bodies are purely artificial fictions beholden to ruling families. The only persons who have billions to invest in these new pyramids are related or closely those connected to those ruling families. Michael Corleone's Mafia crime family pales in comparison to these Middle East oil oligarchies, which have their own tribal codes of loyalty, justice and silence, a morality that boasts its own "whacking" policy against Muslims who "rat" on Mohammed or take Allah's name in vain, or who abandon the tribe completely, and an inbred contempt for and mistrust of all non-Muslim outsiders.

A similar arrangement exists in Mainland China, in which most of the cadres of the ruling Communist Party own and control the "private enterprises" behind China's own economic boom. That arrangement is by definition fascist, and accounts for the censorship, brutal repression, and absence of any civil liberties there. In Saudi Arabia and its Islamic neighbors, the arrangement is much more primitive, and intractably religious.

Such as Prince al-Walid bin Talal, planner of the mile-high tower, who bought the prestigious Savoy Hotel in London for £1.25 billion in 2005, reports the London *Daily Mail* of March 31. Bin Talal is the Saudi who offered former Mayor Rudy Giuliani a $10 million check after the World Trade Center was destroyed by fellow Saudis in 2001. Giuliani promptly returned the check. Bin Talal also is an enabler of Islam in the West, building dozens of mosques in it every year and giving $20 million to Harvard and Georgetown Universities to establish schools of "Islamic studies."

One can imagine bin Talal's mile-high tower is his extravagant way of giving a Bronx cheer to the U.S., the World Trade Center, and all those who died in the attack. Two British firms, Hyder Consulting and Arup, will tackle the tower project in a joint venture with bin Talal's firm, Kingdom Holdings. One supposes that is a kind of reward to the British for wanting to de-emphasize the Holocaust and the Crusades, or not teach the subjects at all, in history lessons in the presence of British Muslim students, for allowing Islamic Sharia law to creep up to equivalence with British secular law, and for many other concessions to Muslim "sensibilities."

Saudi Arabia is the world's biggest oil exporter. "The Persian Gulf countries reaped "$1.5 trillion in oil revenue from 2002 to 2006," reports the *Times* article. Saudi Arabia and its religious/political rival, Iran, another oil exporter, together are the chief enablers of Islamic jihad against the West.

But vertical pyramids and other vanity projects are not the sole means employed by billionaire Arabs to engineer a hostile takeover of the West. The *Times* article reports that,

> "Last year…a fund controlled by the government of Abu Dhabi bought a stake in Citigroup for $7.5 billion, while another run by Dubai's ruler bought a large share in Sony, the Japanese consumer electronics giant. Sabie, a major Saudi petrochemical company, bought the plastics division of General Electric for $11.6 billion, and the Kuwait Petroleum Corporation bought half of Dow Chemical's commodity-plastics unit for $9.5 billion….In recent weeks, other big banks plagued by losses from the mortgage crisis, like Merrill Lynch and Morgan Stanley, have raised tens of billions of dollars from a variety of Middle Eastern and Asian funds, including ones from Kuwait and Saudi Arabia."

The American Congress for Truth reports an April 1st *Human Events* article, in "America for Sale to Sharia Sovereign Wealth Funds," that

> "In December 2007, Bourse Dubai, the world's first and largest Islamic equity exchange, bought 20% of NASDAQ, the biggest U.S. electronic stock market, and 'rebranded' it as part of Dubai's company. The Bourse also got NASDAQ's 28% of the London Stock Exchange (LSE). In addition, Qatar acquired a 24% LSE stake, giving the two Gulf nations control over nearly 52% of the London exchange. On March 15 [2008], Iran, which now dominates the leading 100 Islamic banks – followed by Saudi Arabia, Malaysia and the UAE – announced plans to list a $90 billion energy holding company on the Dubai International Financial Exchange, which is wholly owned by Bourse Dubai."

This article, incidentally, was co-authored by Rachel Ehrenfeld, an American, who was sued in a British court by Saudi billionaire Khalid Salim bin Mahfouz for writing a book, *Funding Evil: How Terrorism is Financed and How to Stop It*, which, among other things, revealed Mahfouz's role in promoting the Islamic conquest of Britain and Europe. The British court ordered her to pay "$225,000 in damages and legal fees to Mahfouz, as well as apologize and destroy existing copies of her books," according to ACT for America on April 1st. Mahfouz is a professional libel "tourist," or terrorist who prefers to extinguish his victims with costly litigation instead of with planes or bombs on vests or in backpacks.

New York State's Court of Appeals declined to protect her from the alleged defamation suit, claiming it did not have jurisdiction over suits originating overseas, thus jeopardizing the efficacy of First Amendment freedom of speech guarantees in the U.S., while implicitly conceding that Americans could be subject to the libel and defamation laws of other nations. On March 31, the New York State legislature unanimously passed the Libel Terrorism Protection Act, which deemed foreign defamation judgments null and void in New York, home of many publishers and writers. Governor David Paterson is expected to sign it into law.

Mahfouz, however, has already made significant inroads by practicing censorship by lawsuit. The most notorious instance to date was his 2007 suit against Cambridge University Press for publishing *Alms for Jihad*, by J. Millard Burr and Robert O. Collins, also Americans, who detailed how Islamic charities are simply money laundering fronts for terrorists. CUP, as a defendant under British libel law, had to refute the accusations and also limit itself in terms of what evidence it could employ in its defense. Rather than face a sea of Saudi petro-pounds in court costs and legal expenses, which it would probably have been ordered to reimburse Mahfouz, CUP caved in to him, withdrew the book from sale and circulation, agreed to shred all existing copies of it, asked libraries to return their copies to be destroyed, and apologized to Mahfouz.

That whole shameful episode of censorship by lawsuit by Islamic billionaires is reminiscent of the John Wilkes affair of 1763, when Wilkes, a member of the House of Commons, said that the king indeed could do wrong, and was promptly charged with libel by the government and expelled from Parliament. He fought back, however, eventually won over his enemies, and his name became synonymous with freedom of the press.

But, to return to the pyramids and the financial subornation of Western capitalism, what must be understood is that these chunks of ownership cannot be likened to investments by the Al Capone crime syndicate, nor even to a Michael Corleone-style ruse of investing a gang's takings in "legitimate" business (see *The Godfather, Part II,* for that tactic), although the root causes are similar. These are aggressive moves by a united political/religious bloc, Islam, to influence the course of Western civilization by acquiring financial leverage over banks, lending institutions, major corporations and investors, and finally over Western political institutions, solely and ultimately to advance the Islamization of the West.

And, as statist regulations and controls foster the growth of organized crime at home and abroad (resulting in such programs the U.S.-directed "war" against the drug cartel in Colombia and tribal poppy-growing enterprises in Afghanistan), irrational foreign policies have fostered the growth of regimes and tyrannies fundamentally hostile to the West. Western policies permitted Saudi Arabia and other OPEC members to seize private oil producing property, and, in conjunction with that inaction, the West at home established prohibitive controls on the development of oil producing resources as part of environmental and "conservation" policies. This has resulted in the West's perilous dependency on the production whims of OPEC and the transfer of enormous wealth to those regimes and tyrannies.

As Nikita Khrushchev once promised that the Soviet Union would 'bury" the U.S. as an industrial power, Saudi Arabia and its Persian Gulf neighbors are promising to bury the U.S. as a global competitor. Instead of demanding that it acknowledge the "superiority" of communism, they will require that the U.S. become a deferential handmaiden of Islam, if not an Islamic province itself.

Of course, all those billion dollar projects are undertaken on the premise that the U.S. and the West will not commit economic suicide by "going green" or by becoming fascist, that they will remain viable, productive realms. If the U.S experiences an economic collapse, the Treasury notes, mutual funds and other government instruments held by Mideast financiers will be as worthless as the ones owned by private American investors and speculators.

Ancient Egyptian kings and pharaohs built over ninety pyramids to house them at death. The new pyramid builders seek to bury the corpse of the West in their own. No one should doubt that Islam – including its kings, emirs, princes, mullahs, imams, its billionaires, its countless mind-stunted manqués, and its homicidal killers – wishes to eviscerate the West, and especially the U.S.

The U.S. and the West should act now to ensure that those mile-high towers, high- rises, and plants remain empty monuments to larcenous vanity, by rediscovering the necessary virtues of self-preservation and self-interest.

April 2008

The New Pyramid Builders II

If you thought the cosmology of the *Koran* was absurdly irrational and a kind of parody of the Bible's, a meeting of Muslim scientists and clerics recently claimed that the *Koran* contains scientific proofs, among them that Mecca is the center of the earth. As a consequence, reported *BBC News* on April 21, they "have called for the adoption of Mecca time to replace GMT."

"Mecca is the direction all Muslims face when they perform their daily prayers. The call was issued at a conference held in the Gulf state of Qatar under the title: *Mecca, the Center of the Earth, Theory and Practice.* One geologist argued that unlike other longitudes, Mecca's was in perfect alignment to magnetic north. He said the English had imposed GMT on the rest of the world by force when Britain was a big colonial power, and it was about time that changed.

"The underlying belief is that scientific truths were also revealed in the Muslim holy book, and it is the work of scholars to unearth and publicize the textual evidence."

Just as their fundamentalist Christian opposite numbers are "unearthing" and publicizing Biblical explanations for everything, from the true age of the universe to the fate of the dinosaurs to the squirms of bacteria. Actually, Greenwich Mean Time was adopted by international agreement and refined in the 1920s by astronomical scientists from around the world. Force had nothing to do with it. But perhaps the most bizarre news from Qatar is the announcement of a special Muslim watch.

"The meeting also reviewed what has been described as a Mecca watch, the brainchild of a French Muslim. The watch is said to rotate anti-clockwise and is supposed to help Muslims determine the direction of Mecca from any point on Earth."

This must earn a special reward for sheer irrationality. But, the "scientific" conference of Muslims is evidence of the hubris Islamists are experiencing as they throttle and subjugate the West. Christians are not the only mystics who wish to make science the servant of religion.

Moving from backward-running Muslim watches and the *Koran* as the foundation of the Periodic Table of Elements to another species of bizarre but real behavior, Walter Williams of George Mason University, in an April 16th column, "Foreign Trade Angst," wrote:

"The United States is the world's largest recipient of foreign direct investment. According to the Economic Report of the President, in 2004, foreigners owned $5.5 trillion in U.S. assets and had $2.3 trillion in sales. They produced $515 billion of goods and services....According to the Congressional Research Service, in 2006 alone, foreign investors spent $184 billion investing in U.S. businesses and real estate, the highest amount foreign investors have spent since 2000...."

Williams can be forgiven for not noting it – his focus was on the anti-free trade sentiment in the U.S. – but many of those "foreign investors" are Mideast potentates of the Persian Gulf who control what are called "sovereign wealth funds" (SWFs), which total over $1 trillion. An April 12th article on the *MoneyNews* site, "Mideast Wealth Funds Rescue Developers," notes that

"Flush with cash and looking for better-than-modest returns, several Middle East sovereign wealth funds are putting money into carefully selected U.S. real estate ventures.

"The funds, *controlled by their governments of origin*, have already pumped billions of investment dollars into U.S. companies and enterprises, but cash allocations to real estate ventures is a relatively new phenomenon." (*Italics* mine.)

Note that the term "sovereign" means "government" – and the term includes the so-called "personal wealth" of about 50,000 royal family members spread between Saudi Arabia, Abu Dhabi, Qatar and the United Arab Emirates, their particular family heads *being* the government. As for the real meaning of the term "wealth," in the context of OPEC and Arab medievalists, it means "loot." The "loot" is the revenue generated by private Western oil properties which Western governments, particularly those of the U.S., Britain, and France, should never have allowed the Arabs to nationalize or otherwise expropriate from the oil companies. The oil companies, for their part, seeing that their properties were not going to be protected by their respective governments, pragmatically entered into "partnerships" with the tribalist ruling cliques in that region, over the decades expanding and improving the properties and cementing their survival on those partnerships.

Apparently, no Ellis Wyatts or Francisco d'Anconias (industrialist heroes of Ayn Rand's prophetic novel, *Atlas Shrugs*, in which producers go on strike against the looters) were in charge in the 1950's to destroy those seized properties.

Someone might object: All those billions being invested in this country represent money, which, although extorted from us, is being put to legitimately productive use. It's unfortunate that it went to sustain tyrannical and religious regimes, but it is coming back.

However, it is irrelevant that the medievalists are assuming the role of risk takers. The money the medievalists are putting into U.S. companies is money that hypothetically should have gone directly to them without being first diverted to the Mideast. That money would have gone to reward risk-taking stockholders and not to the medievalists to allow them to erect their new pyramids.

The concept of "risk" cannot apply to the medievalists for as long as they have a stranglehold on the West. Regardless of the losses they may experience in their portfolios of government instruments, Treasury notes, private stocks, bonds, and the like, and regardless of the failure or poor performance of companies they may have controlling interests in, their fabulous oil revenues will always be guaranteed – provided the West's economy does not first collapse.

On March 18, *WorldNetDaily* carried an article by Jerome R. Corsi, "U.S. Treasury fears Islamic strings on investments."

> "The U.S. Treasury is struggling with how to handle any political or Islamic ramifications as Persian Gulf sovereign wealth funds look to make substantial investments in capital-poor American banks and securities firms.
>
> "*WND* previously reported sovereign wealth funds in six Persian Gulf countries, including Kuwait, the U.A.E. and Qatar, have now amassed

$1.7 trillion, positioning them for attempts to control major banks and securities firms in the U.S.

"Since the beginning of the year, Dubai and Abu Dhabi, two of the largest U.A.E. states, have been in discussions with the U.S. Treasury, offering reassurances that their investments in U.S. bank and security firms would not impose restrictions usually dictated by Islamic law, commonly known as Sharia."

SWF investments in the genuinely productive Western economies are tantamount to our own federal government buying controlling or minimal interests in private corporations, which technically would be *fascism*. What does the infusion of SWFs in private corporations portend?

- The redirection and/or redistribution of private wealth through taxation. In this instance, the "tax" is the artificially high price of oil charged by OPEC (aside from actual federal and state taxes), which has a near monopoly on oil production as a result of Western-sanctioned expropriations and Western environmental policies. This should be obvious from the news reports that OPEC has refused to increase oil production. The Arabs know they have the West cornered.
- It perpetuates the medievalists' wealth-consuming welfare state, which exists only because of irrational, pragmatic Western policies.
- It perpetuates Western dependency on the medievalists' whims.
- It facilitates the incursion of Islamic jihad, both the "soft" kind through financial and political manipulation, and the "hard" kind of Islamofascist violence, which is funded by especially Mideast money from *all* the Persian Gulf states. (Therefore, we are subsidizing our own decline and ultimate destruction. What did Ayn Rand have to say about the "sanction of the victim?" The principle applies to civilizations as well as to individuals.)

SWFs will not be invested in Exxon's or in any of the other major Western oil companies' exploration and drilling projects in Alaska, the Gulf of Mexico, or on the West Coast, provided they are ever approved by

Washington, not unless they can buy controlling interests in such projects, the better to control oil production.

Do not forget that "trade" with the medievalists is not trade in the normal sense, in which values are exchanged to no party's loss. SWFs are loot, and the looting has lasted as long as it has because of especially American energy and foreign policies. One might speculate on the number of congressmen who are in thrall to the medievalists and who block any proposal to allow oil exploration and drilling in areas that are now environmentally "off limits." It is certain that the sheiks, princes and emirs of the Mideast chuckle or gloat over every victory of the environmentalists in Congress and the White House. They must have danced in the streets when ethanol was mandated by the government, and cheered heartily over the biofuel and "clean energy" programs.

Thus, the looters are encouraged by the West's irrational policies. They, like any other criminals or gangs, are counting on the absence of reason and self-assertion in their victims. This is not to say, however, that the medievalists are aware of these concepts in any explicit form; nor is it to claim that the victims are conscious of the crucial, necessary role they play in their survival. The evidence, based on the pragmatic, short-range policies of Western governments, suggests that they are either ignorant or disdainful of such concepts. They are unable or unwilling to learn that, given the bind in which they have placed their countries, the "practical" is inevitably and inarguably *impractical.*

Overlooked in virtually every discussion of the phenomenon is the political leverage the medievalists can acquire in the West by the redirection of their "wealth." As the Treasury Department article above indicates, even American officials see the potential threat of especially Saudi influence on the character and course of American foreign policy and are meekly asking for assurances from the medievalists that they will not, for example, arm-twist the U.S. into abandoning Israel, or recognize Hamas as a legitimate political party, impose censorship on critics of Islam, or even replace Greenwich Mean Time with Mecca Mean Time.

(Notwithstanding our arms sales to it, the U.S. is not much of an ally of Israel since our current policy is to compel Israel to compromise with its mortal enemies and to "cooperate" and help negotiate the formation of a hostile Palestinian state. The U.S. arms deal with the Saudis is bigger by many more billions of dollars. For the nature of the Saudi threat to the U.S., see my commentary of December 13, 2006, "Our Saudi Foes.")

It is interesting to learn that after 9/11, according to an article on the *Saudi-American Forum* site in September 2003, "The United States Must Not Neglect Saudi Arabian Investment," between that infamous date and the spring of 2002, some $200 billion of Saudi SWFs fled the U.S. In 2003, when the Saudis and other Persian Gulf medievalists saw that the U.S. was not only fighting the wrong enemies, Iraq and Afghanistan, but was going out of its way to assure them that they were not perceived as the true enemies, SWFs began to flow back into the country.

Peppered throughout the article, however, are complaints about "discriminatory" actions taken by Americans objecting to Arab investments, together with cautious warnings and admonitions to the U.S. that unless America does something about individuals and organizations that implicate the Saudis with 9/11 and terrorism in general, not to mention Saudi-funded political activism through front organizations such as CAIR, then the Saudis will withdraw their investments and place them elsewhere.

The author of the article writes that

"...Recently thwarted FDI [foreign direct investment] projects in the United States reveal that organized interest groups have sought to target and derail Saudi investments. Locals who objected to Saudi Arabian investment into their community have made a comparison of legitimate Saudi investments to suspect illegal organizations. One project failed as a small group of activists launched a media campaign accusing [sic, *alleging*?] terrorist ties.

"Many Saudi investors are also concerned about becoming victims of lawsuits. Saudi and other foreign investors with no complicity whatsoever with 9/11 or links to terrorism nevertheless perceive the aggressive efforts of an army of U.S. lawyers and entrenched interest groups to 'link and accuse' foreigners in a broad net of litigation. The threat of becoming ensnared in such lawsuits has been reason enough to avoid long-term investments in U.S. markets. *If plaintiff efforts to freeze and tie up investments in advance of any evidence of guilt succeed, foreign faith in U.S. financial markets will suffer.*" [*Italics* mine to underscore one of the veiled threats.]

The author, Tanya C. Hsu, protesteth too much, very likely under the instructions of her Saudi employers. Note that the Saudis group themselves with other "foreigners," as though they were in the same class with private British, French, or other non-governmental foreign risk takers who have invested money in American companies. Note also that the Saudis pose as "victims" of actions taken by Americans who fear an economic takeover of the U.S. by powers hostile to its republican character, without mentioning proven Saudi complicity in funding terrorism, or Saudi-funded political activist groups such as CAIR, or Saudi "libel tourists" who sue authors and publishers to suppress publication of books that demonstrate the links between Saudi money and terrorist activities.

Gag your citizens, demand the Saudis, scrap the First Amendment, forget 9/11, or we will see to it that you suffer your just desserts.

A *Washington Post* article of February 11, 2002, "Enormous Wealth Spilled Into American Coffers," briefly touches on the political connections between Saudi money and government officials.

> "One American financial institution that has attracted Saudi investments is the Washington-based Carlyle Group, whose principal officers include several members of the Saudis' favorite American government of modern times, the first Bush administration. Its principals, who have made millions of dollars from the firm, include former Office of Management and Budget director Richard Darman, former secretary of state [and now defense secretary] James A. Baker III. Former president George H.W. Bush is also a well-paid advisor to Carlyle. Bush has traveled to Saudi Arabia on Carlyle's behalf." [Carlyle, incidentally, failed at the same time as Bear Sterns in the government-caused sub-prime mortgage debacle.]

No doubt Bush Senior has often visited Saudi Arabia with his $100 million buddy, Bill Clinton, whose presidential library in Arkansas received $10 million in donations from the Saudis and untold millions from other Persian Gulf billionaires. Clinton's own Arab connections are probably greater than what has filtered through the media sieve.

However, *The New York Sun,* in a November 22, 2004 article, "Saudis, Arabs Funneled Millions to President Clinton's Library," provides some details, but not the whole picture, of the Clinton-Arab connection.

> "President Clinton's new $165 million library was funded in part by gifts of $1 million or more each from the Saudi royal family and three Saudi businessmen. The governments of Dubai, Kuwait, and Qatar and the deputy prime minister of Lebanon all also appear to have donated $1 million or more for the archive and museum that opened last week."

In exchange for what? For practicing grand scale political chicanery to enfeeble America and deliver it in a state of dhimmitude to its destroyers.

The *Sun* article also mentions that George H. W. Bush's presidential library received significant Saudi donations, as well. When his son, George W. Bush, begins planning his own presidential library, doubtless it will receive generous Saudi and Persian Gulf donations, especially given his "special" handholding relationship with King Abdullah of Saudi Arabia. But, being bought off by the medievalists is not an exclusively Republican venality, as the Democrats like to claim.

How can the medievalists exercise political power over the U.S.? By having politicians like the Bushes and the Clintons in their pockets, in the White House and outside of it.

What will be the end, the dreadful climax? We can put ourselves in Dagny Taggart's place in Ayn Rand's *Atlas Shrugged,* as she listens to another set of looters express their own ambitions, and imagine the same thing with the appropriate substitutions:

> "Then she saw the answer; she saw the secret premise behind their words. With all of their noisy devotion to the age of science, their hysterically technological jargon, their cyclotrons, their sound rays, these men were moved forward, not by the image of an industrial skyline, but by the vision of that form of existence which the industrialists had swept away – the vision of a fat, unhygienic rajah of India, with vacant eyes staring in indolent stupor out of stagnant layers of flesh, with nothing to do but run precious gems through his fingers and, once in a while, stick a knife into the body of a starved, toil-

dazed, germ-eaten creature, as a claim to a few grains of the creature's rice, then claim it from hundreds of millions of such creatures and thus let the rice grains gather into gems

Or into pyramids in the Mideast deserts. Are Americans willing to starve and toil as environmentally acceptable germ-eaten creatures to help the Islamic rajahs of the Persian Gulf build them? For that is the secret means and end of the wielders of SWFs. It remains to be seen.

But Americans are getting no guidance on the matter from the presidential candidates, none of whom dares raise the subject. The depth of their moral depravity is as great as Jimmy Carter's, who recently laid a wreath of roses on the grave of Yasir Arafat.

*Atlas Shrugged, 1957. New York: Dutton. 35th Anniversary Edition. P. 949

April 2008

Our Saudi Foes

Enough about the Iranian bogeyman, President Mahmoud Ahmadinejad! He is our certifiable enemy. Let's shift our focus for a moment to our venal ally in the "war on terror," Saudi Arabia, his chief rival in the conquest or destruction of the U.S.

Ahmadinejad, addressing a conference in Tehran a year ago, proclaimed that "those who doubt, to those who ask is it possible, or those who do not believe, I say accomplishment of a world without America and Israel is both possible and feasible." The Saudis agree with half that statement; for them, the eradication of Israel is a mutual goal, but it would rather convert the U.S. into an Islamic nation, instead of destroy it.

"Saudis and Iran prepare to do battle over corpse of Iraq," read the headline in the *Sunday Telegraph* (London, December 3), and in a later commentary, "The Sandstorm of Western Confusion," I quoted one interesting paragraph from that article:

> "Saudi Arabia, America's closest ally in the Arab world, is considering backing anti-U.S. insurgents because it is so alarmed that Sunnis in Iraq will be left to their fate – military and political – at the hands of the [Iranian-backed] Shia majority."

How would the Saudis accomplish such backing without alienating the prostituted affections of the Bush administration and the State Department? The Associated Press provided an answer in an article that appeared in the Newport News, Virginia *Daily Press* on December 8th under the headline, "Saudi citizens finance Iraq's Sunni fighters, report says." The report is that of the Iraq Study Group.

> "Private Saudi citizens are giving millions of dollars to Sunni Muslim insurgents in Iraq, and much of it is used to buy weapons, including shoulder-fired [Russian Strela] anti-aircraft missiles, according to key Iraqi officials and others familiar with the flow of cash."

This is an interesting subject in the ISG's report that hasn't received the attention it deserves by the American news media, whose news anchors and Washington correspondents are barely able to contain their joy over the bipartisan recommendations that President Bush abandon the idea of victory in Iraq and begin talking with Iran and Syria with the goal of "stabilizing" the chaos in Iraq.

"Saudi government officials deny that any money from their country is being sent to Iraqis fighting the government and the U.S.-led coalition. But the ISG report said Saudis are a source of money for Sunni Arab insurgents. Several truck drivers interviewed by the Associated Press described carrying boxes of cash from Saudi Arabia into Iraq – money they said was headed for insurgents."

"Two high-ranking Iraqi officials, speaking on condition of anonymity because of the issue's sensitivity, told the AP most of the Saudi money came from private donations, called zaqat, collected for Islamic causes and charities."

The article reports that the Saudis claim to be tracking "suspicious financial operations." Tracking and policing such operations, however, are two distinct actions. The AP article continues, "The ISG report said that 'funding for the Sunni insurgency comes from private individuals within Saudi Arabia and other (Persian) Gulf states.'" Oman? Kuwait? Qatar? Bahrain? The United Arab Emirates?

In the moral dustbowls of all these medieval enclaves, such "private individuals" must have close political and economic connections to their royalist governments to be wealthy enough to indulge in such generosity. Their "charitable" donations must have the tacit approval and knowledge of the powers in the royal palaces and compounds.

As evil and perversely bizarre as the notion is that an alleged American ally would condone or sanction its citizens enabling "insurgents" to kill American soldiers – but not incite the rage of either the Bush administration or the news media or members of the ISG – the Saudis are also funding another kind of insurgency in the U.S. itself. Its chief front organization is the Council on American-Islamic Relations (CAIR).

The goal of this "insurgency" is two-fold: to whitewash Islam by projecting it as a benign creed deserving of special dispensations and treatment vis-à-vis American law; and to insinuate the Islamic ethos into American society with the ultimate goal of transforming it from a secular to an Islamic society (which means discarding the Constitution and replacing it with the *Koran*). Its chief weapons until now have been lawsuits and press releases.

CAIR is a lobby-cum-"civil rights" organization that advances Saudi interests in the U.S. It is staffed by Wahhabists and financially supported by surreptitiously donated Saudi and other "Gulf" money. That is, by American motorists, without their knowledge, at the gas pump.

Now CAIR has allies in Congress. Up to now, it has counted on the gullibility and short-ranged mentalities of the news media and even the White House to lend it an air of innocence and concern. Up to now, the rule has been dinners for Muslim guests at the White House, receptions for them in swank hotels, and a congenial first-name-basis camaraderie.

When Congress reconvenes next year, CAIR and its phalanx of interlinked Muslim organizations in the U.S. will expect their leftist and Democratic allies in the Senate and House to work for and deliver legislation that will protect the Islamic beachhead in America. For a detailed summary of the goals and backgrounds of the "usual suspects" – Nancy Pelosi, John Conyers, and Keith Ellison – see Robert Spencer's article, "CAIR's Congress" in *FrontPageMagazine* of November 13, 2006; Robert Novak's article in the *Chicago Sun-Times* of December 10 on Zalmay Khalilzad, the outgoing U.S. ambassador to Iraq and a Muslim who will likely become the U.S. envoy at the United Nations; and "John Conyers and the Muslim Caucus" in the *Investor's Business Daily* of November 9.

More disturbing, however, is another article from the December 4th *FrontPageMagazine*, "CAIR KOs '24'," by Henry Mark Holzer.

> "Early in 2005, CAIR met with representatives of the Fox television network and producers of the hit drama '24' to discuss concerns about the depiction of a 'Muslim' family at the heart of a terror plot on that popular program," cites Holzer from CAIR's Annual Report, titled "The Status of Muslim Civil Rights in the United States 2006, The Struggle for Equality." "CAIR was concerned that the portrayal of the family as a terrorist 'sleeper cell' would cast suspicion over ordinary American Muslims and increase Islamophobia.

> "Rabiah Ahmed, spokeswoman for CAIR, said that the show was 'taking everyday American Muslim families and making them suspects. It's very dangerous and very disturbing."

CAIR's Annual Report continues:

> "At the meeting, which included CAIR and the Muslim Public Affairs Council (MPAC), Fox officials agreed to distribute a CAIR public service announcement to network affiliates and ask that it be aired in proximity to '24.' Network officials also agreed to air a disclaimer stating the American Muslims reject terrorism."

Mr. Holzer writes:

> "Although many Americans were rightly enraged at Fox's capitulation to CAIR, they wrongly complained of 'censorship.'" Holzer, Professor Emeritus at Brooklyn Law School, correctly counters that Fox's submission – and remember that "Islam" means "submission" – did

not constitute censorship. "Only the government has the power to censor (subject to whatever protection that might be afforded by the federal First Amendment and state constitutions)."

What Fox's decision did constitute was: cowardice.

CAIR insisted that Kiefer Sutherland, who plays the intrepid Jack Bauer, a counterterrorism agent, issue the politically correct version of a parental guidance warning: *"...Now while terrorism is obviously one of the most critical challenges facing our nation and the world, is important to recognize that the American Muslim community stands firmly beside their fellow Americans in denouncing and resisting all forms of terrorism. So in watching '24,' please, bear that in mind."*

Which Sutherland did. Technically, it was called a "disclaimer." What it disclaims and abdicates, however, is the right of Fox in "24" to portray Muslims as it sees fit, regardless of the accuracy of such a portrayal, regardless of the fact that most American Muslims are an alien fifth column of manqués, conditioned by the *Koran* and their clerics to do the bidding of Allah, Mohammad, and CAIR. CAIR's Annual Report could just as well have been titled, "The Status of Muslim Civil Rights in the United States 2006, The Struggle for Supremacy."

Holzer then lets fly at CAIR:

"Wrapping itself in the flag, invoking the Constitution, and hiding beneath its veneer of a self-styled 'civil liberties' organization – modeled on its anti-American mentor and template, the American Civil Liberties Union – CAIR is the preeminent domestic mailed fist of Islam in the velvet glove of civil liberties....CAIR is using the American legal system to intimidate the exercise of free speech, to undermine our homeland defense and to advance Muslim cultural infiltration of our domestic institutions by seeking special dispensations concerning dress, national holidays, educational texts, the content of books, movies, television, and more. In addition to its incessant intimidating complaints about the alleged violation of 'Muslim Civil Liberties.'"

(The balance of Holzer's article is a description of the extent of CAIR's legal activism in the U.S., to which the news media and our elected representatives are either oblivious or criminally ambivalent.)

While Fox's decision to "submit" to Islamic sensibilities indeed does not constitute censorship (see Ayn Rand's definition and discussion of censorship in *The Ayn Rand Lexicon*), it is symptomatic of what could be called "mirror censorship," that is, self-censorship from fear and moral cowardice without the excuse of being subjected to or threatened with government force. In the fog-bound ethics of approximations, relativism, and non-absolutes, the one absolute that pragmatists, "realists" and the "practical" fear to encounter in that fog is: the necessity of opposing censorship. Censorship is the forcible suppression of free speech by the entity that has a monopoly on force, the government. Facing naked censorship, they know they must take a moral stand.

So one must wonder about the moral stature of men who readily submit to *faux* force, that is, to the whims and wishes of a "community" that threatens lawsuits, demonstrations, or boycotts. Since force is not threatened, the pragmatists and "realists" feel comfortable by acknowledging a group's "displeasure" and claims of "persecution" and by calling their penance "public service." One cannot but conclude that they would rather not face a moral decision at all, and that, confronted with genuine censorship, they would sanction that, as well, in the name of the "public good."

Let us not forget the power behind CAIR, which is chiefly Saudi money. That money has been funding gangs of tribalist killers who target American soldiers in Iraq, as well as funding "civil liberties" insurgents in this country who target the First Amendment. And now the Baker-Hamilton team of compromisers is proposing that the U.S. hold direct talks with Iran and Syria, which have also been sending money and weapons to Iraq to kill American soldiers.

One of Bush's gravest errors was not asking Congress for a declaration of war against the "axis of evil." As a friend explained, such a declaration would give the U.S. the right to deem an organization like CAIR an enemy agent and to take the appropriate wartime punitive actions. But no such declaration has been made; one consequence of that failure is that the moral behavior of private individuals and organizations like Fox has too often mirrored that of our foreign policy: cowardice and appeasement. Remember the Danish cartoon imbroglio?

At least American soldiers can fight back and kill the enemy in Iraq. But where, Holzer asks, are the "dedicated lawyers with the desire to meet CAIR on the legal battlefield...?" Are they all dead? Are they too busy passing statist legislation in Congress, such as the selective censorship of the Campaign Finance Law, or cooking up class action suits against businesses?

In *Book Four – Empire* of my *Sparrowhawk* series, Patrick Henry, a lawyer and freshman burgess, about to introduce his Stamp Act Resolves in the Virginia General Assembly in May of 1765, states:

> "We propose that this House adopt and forward to those parties [Parliament and King George the Third], not genuflective beseechments or adulatory objurgations, but pungent resolves of our understanding of the origins and practice of British and American

liberty, resolves which will frankly alert them to both the error of their presumptions and our determination to preserve that liberty. These resolves, in order to have some consequence and value, ought not to be expressed by us in the role of effusive mendicants applying for the restitution of what has been wrested from them, but with the cogently blunt mettle of men who refuse to be robbed."

The historical irony is that when Henry made his speech, the Wahhabist Saudis were engaged in the conquest of the Arabian Peninsula, which they completed in 1806. Who could have predicted then that their descendents and their hired *fellaheen* would invade America two and half centuries later with the express purpose of gagging the likes of Henry in the name of Allah?

December 2006

Somali Piracy: Another Islamic War Front

On February 22nd, four Americans were executed by Somali pirates as a U.S. warship bore down on the yacht they had hijacked. The U.S. government and the military are not saying much about why the pirates killed the Americans, but it just might have something to do with the fact that the two retired couples were on a private missionary voyage around the world to distribute Bibles in Third World villages and spread Christianity. All Somali pirates are Muslims. Very likely, even after having command of the yacht for three days and in the midst of negotiations for the hostages' release, it had something to do with the Bibles the pirates found on board the yacht.

On Tuesday, Somali pirates shot and killed four American hostages. A single hostage intentionally killed by these pirates had been almost unheard of; four dead was unprecedented....

Exactly what happened Tuesday is still murky. Pirates in the Arabian Sea had hijacked a sailboat skippered by a retired couple from California, and when the American Navy closed in, the pirates got twitchy. Navy Seals rushed aboard but it was too late. It's still not clear why the pirates would want to kill the hostages when their business model, which has raked in more than $100 million in the past few years, is based on ransoming captives alive.

But I suspect that if the pirates had instead found cartons of Playboy Magazine on the yacht, the Americans would have suffered the same fate. It would demonstrate the grip Islam has even on criminal Muslims.

It is unlikely that the pirates expected to collect much of a ransom from the murdered Americans. It is likely that they were holding the U.S. government hostage, by demanding *it* pay the pirates the ransom instead. Two of the pirates were aboard the warship "negotiating" when pirates on the yacht fired at the warship, and then gunfire on the yacht itself was heard.

The big money is in hijacking commercial vessels, such as super-tankers and super-cargo ships, and holding them and their crews hostage until ransoms are paid. Because of the murders, however, I believe the Somali pirates have adopted a new tactic: kidnap smaller private vessels whose owners are unlikely to be able to pay million dollar ransoms, and hold the captured nationals on them hostage until their governments pay up.

The pirates have sent an unmistakable message to the U.S. and other Western governments: they mean business. Does the U.S. mean business? Is it willing to pay millions in "tribute" to Islamic pirates (a.k.a. Islamic *jizya*) as Americans were not willing to pay Napoleon to stop raiding American vessels? The hijacking of a private Danish yacht several days ago suggests this new strategy. The promise to execute the Danes, a mother, father, their three teenage children, and two other adults if a rescue attempt is made, suggests this new tactic, as well.

Most hostages captured in the pirate-infested waters off East Africa are professional sailors. Pirates rarely capture families and children, but a 3-year-old boy was aboard a French yacht seized in 2009. His father was killed in the rescue operation by French navy commandos. Two pirates were killed and four French citizens were freed, including the child.

The Danish family was captured along with two adult crew members, also Danes, when their sailboat was seized by pirates Thursday, the Danish government said.

Mohamed [a spokesman for the pirates] said that any attack against the pirates would result in the deaths of the hostages, and he referred to the killings last week of four American hostages captured by pirates on their yacht.

Jihad Watch reports on the natural and logical connection between Islamic jihadists and the pirates, who, being Muslims waging war on the West, act as a kind of guerilla contingent. But this is not officially acknowledged. The West dare not convict or indict Islam, lest Islamists cry foul. But Somali Jihadists are now demanding their cut of any ransoms paid, and the cut is strictly by the book – the *Koran*.

> "And know that whatever ye take as spoils of war, lo! a fifth thereof is for Allah, and for the messenger and for the kinsman (who hath need) and orphans and the needy and the wayfarer, if ye believe in Allah and that which We revealed unto Our slave on the Day of Discrimination, the day when the two armies met. And Allah is Able to do all things."
> — Qur'an 8:41

The West, however, is not able to do anything. Its hands are tied by a fear of offending Muslims by naming the moral culprit. It refuses to acknowledge that the pirates are proxy allies of the jihadists. It prefers to treat the pirates as mere criminals.

The piracy "crisis" off the Somali coast can be solved easily and quickly – the West certainly has the means to do so – but with some regrettable risks and consequences. The situation, after all, is of the West's own making. Western governments have dithered and bitten its nails for years over what to do, not only because the pirates still hold ships and hostages, but because the pirates are Muslims.

That is what is stopping any concerted action – such as blasting every pirate ship and every pirate port and safe havens to atoms, and shooting to kill on sight any pirate with no chance of "trial" in any Western nation. When pirates were captured in the West ages ago, they were summarily tried and hanged.

"But," one might object, "they'll just execute the hostages or they'll be killed during an attack. That isn't very humane. It's better to just dither and negotiate. To attack the pirates would be barbarous, especially because they aren't as well-armed as we are. What would the world think?"

It is not bad enough that "Just War" theory reigns supreme in our military. It apparently reigns supreme when dealing with gangs of pirates.

During World War Ii, when the Allies decided to bomb German and Japanese cities to accelerate the surrender of the Nazis and the Japanese and to bring the war closer to an end, doubtless strategists knew that some "innocent" German and Japanese civilians would be killed as well as those who actively or complicitly supported and sanctioned the Nazi and Imperialist regimes. When American bombers attacked Japanese cities, they also did so knowing that American POW's were being used as slave labor in those cities, and that they, too, might be killed.

This is also a risk the West must take with the pirates' hostages if it is ever going to erase the pirate jihadists off the map. The moral conundrum is possible only because the West has refused to acknowledge the nature and identity of its enemy: Islam. The piracy "problem" is a direct consequence of especially the U.S.'s "war on terror." It is a direct consequence of not eliminating states that sponsor terrorism.

What is the alternative? Allowing the hostages to remain in captivity until they rot away, or are killed because no ransom was collected or likely to be collected, and perpetuating the commissions of crime on the high seas. Is not acting decisively against the pirates a more humane policy? Is allowing the hostage sailors to remain hostages, still living at the whim of killers, who are now resorting to torturing the hostages, a more humane policy? No.

I am sure that Western governments have every Somali pirate port and village pinpointed. It should simply give a single warning, broadcast to the pirates, that all hostages are to be released, unharmed, immediately, and all hijacked vessels abandoned by the pirates. If all we got in reply were threats to kill the hostages, or actual executions, or if they reply with a wish to "negotiate," Western naval vessels should simply commence erasing the ports, the villages, and every pirate vessel afloat; the "mother ships" especially should be sunk as well, and no attempt made to rescue survivors. Let the sharks claim them. No mercy should be shown to any pirate. The Somali pirates show none for Westerners or anyone they take hostage. Remember the four Americans executed by them just a few weeks ago?

Would this action violate the sovereignty of Somalia? No. There is no such country as Somalia. It is a region of anarchy with no true government, and one to which the U.S, incredibly, is paying to simply exist, with no power to punish the pirates.

Somalia's central government collapsed more than 20 years ago, and now its landscape includes droughts, warlords, fighters allied to Al Qaeda, and malnutrition, suffering and death on a scale unseen just about anywhere else.

The United States and other Western powers are pouring millions of dollars into Somalia's transitional government, an appointed body with little legitimacy on the ground, in the hope, perhaps vain, that it can rebuild the world's most failed state and create an economy based on something like fishing or livestock. Young men then might be able to earn a living doing something other than sticking up ships.

The Times aptly describes the kind of country Somalia is:

> Piracy Inc. is a sprawling operation on land, too. It offers work to tens of thousands of Somalis — middle-managers, translators, bookkeepers, mechanics, gunsmiths, guards, boat builders, women who sell tea to pirates, others who sell them goats. In one of the poorest lands on earth, piracy isn't just a business; it's a lifeline.

It is time the West extinguished that bandits' economy and to severed the lifeline, but enacted no Marshall Plan to help Somalia back to its economic and political feet. Victims do not owe their subdued victimizers anything.

Remember that the Somali pirates are Muslims and that they are obeying the commands of the *Koran*. During WWII, the Allies did not stay their hand because they could point to some "benign" passages in *Mein Kampf.* The Somali coast is as much a war front as Western Europe was during WWII. But the West must first acknowledge that Islam has declared war on the West, and that the Islamic jihadists have declared war on it and make no distinction between military and civilian targets. Or were the World Trade Center and the Pentagon, and the London subway, and the Madrid train station, and the Bali resort, et al., all figments of our imagination?

The Somali pirates hold between 600 and 800 hostages, and still have under their guns between 50 and 80 vessels of various sizes, some of which they have converted into "mother ships" that can range far beyond Somali's coast to launch "swift boats" to attack private vessels and commercial shipping. The sea lanes between the Gulf of Aden and in the Arabian Sea have become "seize lanes."

The West has the air power, the firepower and the navies in place to accomplish the end of Somali piracy. All it needs are the will and the moral certainty to get on with it.

And while we are on the subject of thievery and extortion, one must ask: Is there any difference between Somali piracy and, say, Saudi, Libyan, or Venezuelan extortion of Western wealth in oil in the Western oil fields developed by Western companies? Somalis are not the only pirates. The entire membership of OPEC is a club of pirates, extortionists, and thieves – of Western wealth.

At the very least, a military strike against the Somali pirates would send a clear message to Islamist jihadists everywhere: This particular reign of terror is over. One should wholeheartedly agree with William R. Hawkins when he stresses that it is the pirates, like any criminal who initiates force, who should be mindful of the risks, chiefly that they may forfeit their lives if retaliatory force is employed.

It is a strategic mistake to appease aggressors. It is the pirates who must be put at risk, and learn the harsh lesson that their raids will only result in their own destruction.

And punitive attacks against pirates should not mean "nation building" or any prolonged involvement in the country. Indeed, any deep intervention in a place as wild as Somalia is to be avoided. The mission would simply be to teach the brigands that "crime" doesn't pay with an application of armed might beyond anything they can imagine or endure.

It the West cannot or will not deal with so lesser a threat as pirates, then it is doomed to extinction, and the Islamists will have won.

March 2011

The Sandstorm of Western Confusion

One of the most foolish squibs I have ever read outside of State Department pap on how to deal with Islam and Muslims appeared in the *Daily Telegraph* (London) on November 30th. Michael Burleigh, author and distinguished visiting fellow at the Hoover Institution at Stanford University, in "Winning Muslim hearts and minds," argues that a key factor in successfully combating terrorism and Muslim "separatism" in Western nations is to somehow communicate with "moderate," non-violent Muslims. "Let's reach out to them," writes Burleigh, "or at least create some forum where we can be reminded of their existence."

> "Rather, we lazily allow Islamist fundamentalists to equate our culture with trashy television programs about penile implants rather than Bach, Rubens or Mozart, Newton, Pascal or Einstein. As the philosopher Roger Scruton has written, we should be more careful about what image (and reality) of ourselves we project into more traditional societies."

Translation: We should strive to assure "moderate" Muslims that we are not "profiling" their barbarous creed, and that we really don't believe the jihadists and suicide bombers and ranting imams among them are practicing that creed in its most fundamental terms or are in the least representative of Islam in its ideal state.

Given that Europe is now populated with about 50 million Muslims, I don't think anyone needs to be reminded of their existence. They have invaded and invested Europe, and have established a foothold in the U.S. Their agent provocateurs here are busy testing the legal waters to see if this country is as weak and accommodating as Europe. They are fashioning nooses with which to hang us from the hemp of multiculturalism and tolerance.

(For an excellent appraisal of Europe's future prospects vis-à-vis the Muslim Borg, articulated by German author Henryk M. Broder, see "The Rape of Europe" by Paul Belien in *The Brussels Journal* of October 25th.)

Conceding that contemporary Western culture is predominantly "trashy" – a appellation that can be applied to most modern art, literature, and music, as well as to television – what would be gained by projecting a better "image" to insular tribal societies such as that of the Muslims? It can't be that Muslim rank-and-file or their fire and brimstone clerics care a fig about Bach, Rubens, Newton or Einstein. Islamists wish to conquer and eliminate the civilization that produced such creators and thinkers. Islam in its "at rest" state is a model of smug, conscientious, cultural stagnancy. It has no room for, and can never produce, the likes of Michelangelo or Jonas Salk. Islam makes no distinction between the Rolling Stones and Berlioz. In Islam's miasmatic, anti-life ethos, all such Western values are decadent and corrupting.

In response to Burleigh's proposed policy of patronizing vacillation, I posted a comment in the reader's column that more or less said:

> It is not possible to win the "hearts and minds" of dedicated, or even semi-dedicated Muslims. Islam is one of the most "heartless" of religions. It tolerates good will among only Muslims, and even then it is conditional. As for kaffirs and other non-believers, it is open season on them at the whim of Islam's clerics and rulers.

And as for "minds," Islam is more hostile to them than is Christianity. It is a "God says so because Mohammad said so" faith from top to bottom. This is why one rarely hears from "moderate" Muslims. They are caught between allegiance to the rational and allegiance to the utter irrationality of Islamic tenets and dictates, their convictions divided between remaining loyal to Allah and heeding Mohammad and being loyal to some semblance of wanting to live on earth (just as many Christians are, but much more pathologically).

Unlike Christians, devout Muslims can't pigeonhole their religious beliefs and get on with life. Unlike Christians, they can't spend one morning in mosque and then live on earth the rest of the week without so much as a nod to Mecca; Islam requires their daily expression of submission. Understand the ubiquitous presence of Big Brother in Orwell's "Nineteen Eighty-Four" and what the totalitarian Party expected of its members – which was unswerving, unthinking, *goodthink* obedience in all things – and you will understand Islam and Muslims.

So, it is futile to attempt to persuade Muslims that theirs is a fatal dichotomy, and to boast of all the wonderful things Western culture has produced and which they, too, can share and appreciate. Reason is the enemy of faith, not its occasional handmaiden (the assertions of Pope Benedict to the contrary notwithstanding), and the truly faithful of any creed are beyond rational persuasion. Since a Muslim possesses the attribute of volition, it is he who must exercise it (and a very, very few have).

I could have added: And they don't care, either. If the works of Beethoven, Shakespeare, or Newton were to suddenly perish, or the statue of David in Florence or the Statue of Liberty was blown to bits by "disenchanted" fellow Muslims, do you think we would witness "moderate" Muslim men and women in Baghdad or Dearborn or London's East End writhing and wailing in hysterical grief? Not likely.

An interesting post followed in the *Daily Telegraph* on December 1st, in apparent answer to Burleigh's encomium on reciprocity and "reaching out." There was no attribution or credit; it simply appeared on its own page, under the same title. Its theme is that the West should not rush to win Muslim "hearts and minds" when Muslims are the victims of natural disasters, such as the recent Indonesian tsunami and the Pakistani quake.

> "...When such a calamity strikes a Muslim population, whom are we trying to rescue? We are rescuing our future murderers. The suicide bombers on the London Tube came from Pakistan. [Actually, they were British citizens of Pakistani origin.] They were the kin of those whom we rescued in Muzafarrabad." [Actually, their more animated spiritual kin.]

Although much of the anonymous post is rambling, it does make a few trenchant observations and draws some legitimate parallels. The best one is this:

> "Muslims have always attacked those of their adversaries who have been struck by a natural disaster. When a sandstorm struck a Sassanid Persian army at the battle of Quadisiya in modern day Iraq, the Arab Muslim attackers took full advantage of that Persian discomfiture and slaughtered the entire retreating Persian army."

A little research provided some historical context which the anonymous writer did not establish. The Persian Sassanian Dynasty established an empire in the Mideast between AD 244 and 651, most of which fell to Arab conquerors in 640. Mohammad died in 632, and until then was battling for Arabia, so he can't be blamed for that particular conquest, although his followers can be, busy as they were spreading the faith by sword. The Quadisiya sandstorm debacle probably occurred in the reign of Khosrow II, the last Sassanian king, who died in 628. On his death, the empire quickly disintegrated and became easy pickings for Mohammad's followers. Its capital, Ctesiphon, was taken by them in 637.

Elsewhere in the article, the anonymous writer recommends that the West adopt the same Islamic tactic that has been used against the West, even to the point of adapting the Islamic ultimatum: Abandon Islam, or die. He more or less has the same advice that another correspondent proffered, to wit, that if Mecca and the Kaaba were reduced to molten glass and tens of thousands of pebble-throwing pilgrims vaporized in a small nuclear detonation, nothing would happen. Allah, who does not exist, would neither prevent the attack nor avenge it.

Countless Muslims worldwide would subsequently experience such a crisis of faith that most would adjure Islam. And that would be the end of that. The "war on terror" would be won. As my correspondent noted, this recommendation also came from an ex-Muslim. "The fellow who suggested it was adamant that this would indeed demoralize the Muslim world and convince them that they are not going to inherit the earth."

Nuking Mecca, Medina, Riyadh, Damascus, and Tehran to demoralize Muslims would be an exercise in preemption, certainly heartless but one way of appealing to minds otherwise insensate to reason by way of the primary goal of defending ourselves. After all, Ahmadinejad is promising us the same apocalyptic destruction.

By all available evidence, however, our political leaders are staring straight into the sandstorm of pragmatism, appeasement, wishful thinking, and diplomacy. Taking the moral high ground in a preemptive strike against our enemies is not in the cards. Neither President Bush, nor Secretary of State Rice, nor Prime Minister Tony Blair, nor the Iraq Study Group, nor any European leader can take a moral high ground. They are all value-negating multiculturalists. Since the moral is to defend and preserve a value, their minds are shut to the necessity of defending any Western value.

And while our leaders are being blinded by a sandstorm of their own making, thinking they are constructing a Roman aqueduct when they are actually digging a shallow ditch, our enemies are not only chortling over the dilemma in which the U.S. finds itself in Iraq – an occupation to win Muslim "hearts and minds" by not fighting a true war – but preparing to fight over the spoils. The Persians and the Arabs are again maneuvering to contest control of Iraq. "Saudis and Iran prepare to do battle over corpse of Iraq," reads the headline of the *Sunday Telegraph* (December 3).

> "In Tehran, Iranian leaders have made clear that they believe they are the big winners from America's involvement in Iraq. 'The kind of service that the Americans, with all their hatred, have done us – no superpower has ever done anything similar,' Mohsen Rezal, secretary-general of the powerful Expediency Council that advises the Supreme Leader Ayatollah Khamanei, boasted on state television recently."

In the meantime:

> "Saudi Arabia, America's closest ally in the Arab world, is considering backing anti-U.S. insurgents because it is so alarmed that Sunnis in Iraq will be left to their fate – military and political – at the hands of the [Iranian-backed] Shia majority." Vice President Dick Cheney flew to Riyadh last week to discuss the matter.

An ally so close that he can stick a dagger in our hearts – again. It isn't enough that the Saudis can hold the U.S. hostage with its confiscated oil wealth and produce suicide bombers with which to attack our cities. Now they want to pay "insurgents" to kill American soldiers. I suspect they have been doing this all the while, helping to bankroll Sunni "freedom fighters" in Iraq, and that the Bush administration has known it all the while. But, in the rarefied, oxygen-short realms of diplomacy, it isn't tactful to identify or acknowledge a truth. Two plus two can be any sum one wishes, and somehow translate into "stability" on the ground.

In the meantime, there is to be a "meeting of minds."

"…In a break with previous policy, Mr. Bush will meet tomorrow in Washington with Abdul Aziz al-Hakim, head of the Supreme Council for the Islamic Revolution in Iraq, a party closely tied to Iran."

That, one supposes, to paraphrase Mr. Burleigh, is the political way of "somehow communicating with moderate, non-violent Muslims." Only it is the Islamists who are reminding Bush of their existence. The last vestige of Bush's moral stature, such as it was, has gone up in a little puff of smoke.

Stay tuned, if you can stomach it. The sandstorm can only get worse.

December 2006

The Perils of a Siege Mentality

What bothers me endlessly about the Transportation Security Administration (TSA) and the Department of Homeland Security (DHS) is that they operate on the policy that defeat by our enemies is implicitly conceded. That is the policy adopted by our government, and one can trace it all the way back to President Ronald Reagan's failure to retaliate against the murder of nearly 250 Marines in their bunker-like barracks in Lebanon in 1983 and the policy that sent them there. Instead of striking a mortal blow at Iran and Hezbollah, we indulged in a wave of maudlin mourning and shameful self-pity.

The policy of defeat, however, is made possible by a variety of factors, not least of which are the philosophy of multiculturalism, a refusal to identify and strike against our enemies (that is, a refusal to ascribe evil to the advocates of the philosophy that motivates them), and, in the context of a government dedicated to expanding its powers under both Republican and Democratic administrations, a penchant for control at all costs, including the sacrifice of freedom. Tyrannies, dictatorships, and authoritarian regimes have no concern about the loss of freedom. Freedom is their enemy. It is not on their checklists of things to preserve and protect. Freedom is antithetical to control.

The TSA is deserving of every bit of criticism it has earned, both as a functioning bureaucracy and as a product of government policies. It is staffed by thousands of careless, indiscriminate, prostituting, ignorant drones. I no longer consider them as Americans, but as an alien presence in our midst, as alien as the mindless followers of Islam. So, please, no one remind me or any other liberty-loving American that they are just "doing their job" or that they do not establish policy, or that they are just "following orders." That's the Nuremberg trial defense. Every nation at any period of its history has its population of dross and ballast – even during the American Revolution – and the TSA is a natural magnet for the ones in this country.

But the TSA is merely a handmaiden of the DHS, and the DHS is but an ossified expression of a suicidal policy that has been germinating for decades. It is purely reactive in nature. It has accepted the overall policy of a state of siege as a normal, permanent mode of this country's existence. The government does not bear the burden of such a policy, but rather its citizens. That policy will not strike a mortal blow at our enemies – Saudi Arabia, Iran, Syria, Libya, Yemen, and the lesser regimes – so it must adopt a state of siege mentality. Osama bin Laden knew his enemy, we must credit him with the observation that neither George W. Bush nor Barack Obama would acknowledge and act against Islamic states as the enemy, but instead adopt the futile policy of appeasement and a state of siege.

As part of the "bleed-until-bankruptcy plan," bin Laden cited a British estimate that it cost al Qaeda about $500,000 to carry out the attacks of

September 11, 2001, an amount that he said paled in comparison with the costs incurred by the United States. "Every dollar of al Qaeda defeated a million dollars, by the permission of Allah, besides the loss of a huge number of jobs," he said. As for the economic deficit, it has reached record astronomical numbers estimated to total more than a trillion dollars. The total U.S. national debt is more than $7 trillion. The U.S. federal deficit was $413 billion in 2004, according to the Treasury Department.

A government that will not acknowledge an external enemy of "the people" must regard "the people" as its potential enemy. Its capacity for aggression, if not directed against a legitimate enemy, will be directed against a nation's civilian population. Witness now the energy it is expending to control the speech of its citizens via the Federal Communications Commission through its incipient control of the Internet. "Net neutrality" is just a euphemism for neutering the power of ideas.

Two consequences are ensured by such a state of siege policy: the establishment of a police state that monitors and regulates every action and thought of the citizens of this country (this is beside the domestic policy of adopting socialized medicine through ObamaCare, and other instances of destructive and parasitical Democratic legislation); and the continued assault on this country by its enemies. A government that will not order its military to open its gates and storm out to assault the besiegers, is doomed to capitulation and defeat. What is holding us back? In 2002 former Secretary of Defense Caspar Weinberger was interviewed about the Marine barracks massacre. He was asked why President Reagan did not order a military response. He answered, quoting Reagan:

> "Almost any target we attack will have huge collateral damage." Collateral damage is the polite way of phrasing the number of innocent women and children who are killed because you're engaging in a war, and it was up in the hundreds of thousands.

But a concern about "collateral damage" was not our policy while waging war against Nazi Germany and Imperial Japan. If it had been, World War II would have lasted decades or even have been lost – just as the current "war against terrorism" has lasted a decade and is being lost. Weinberger also made this revealing observation about Reagan:

> He said he simply did not want to trust the future of the world to philosophic assumptions.

There you have it. Philosophical bankruptcy, even "on principle," necessarily means moral bankruptcy. Instead, Reagan, Bush, and to a lesser extend President Obama, cite "tradition," God, and other irrelevant issues as reasons to "resist" Islamic jihadists, but not to exterminate their root. That would be "judgmental," and moral judgments are prohibited in an environment of "moral equivalency."

So, discussions such as the Washington Post's cogitations about the efficacy of airport body scanners and intrusive pat-downs are superfluous but indicative of how far this country has declined as a free one, and how far the government is prepared to go to establish a permanent police state. In the broad picture of things, such an article is useless speculation and complicit in a trend to "condition" Americans to being answerable to the state. In the country of the self-blinded, the one-eyed man is king because he has a purpose and an insidious method and can see where he is going.

Reading this cold, dispassionate discussion in the Washington Post of how better to establish a police state, one realizes that this is now a country that would prefer to live in a state of siege, rather than eliminate the countries that sponsor terrorism and that have attacked us by proxy with foreign and American-born or naturalized terrorists.

What bothers me just as much is also the willingness of Americans to tolerate and endure the airport terminal as a police state. There is no fundamental difference between conscientiously filling out a 1099 and an IRS audit, and removing one's shoes, belts and jewelry and submitting to a body scan or a pat-down, except in its immediacy. Obey, or suffer the consequences. So, let us suggest here that, for example, the omnipotent IRS, as one controlling agency, has conditioned Americans to that kind of treatment, to sanction the hostage-taking of their values and to concede that they are but the wards of a guardian government.

The Tea Party movement to the contrary notwithstanding, Americans are behaving more and more like sheep willing to be sheared. They need to be taught that such shearing leaves them naked before the government and all its eager, groping minions, and a laughing stock of our external enemies, who will continue killing us as they snort in triumph.

Sheared, shivering, and going about their government-approved business, laden with computerized ankle or wrist bracelets, too many Americans will assure themselves that they will feel "safe." They will be told that surrendering their freedom is the "price of freedom."

Contradictions do not exist in reality, except in human action and within one's mind. That is a perilous, suicidal mode of existence.

December 2010

Of Piracy and Politics

The Associated Press reported on January 11th what was otherwise an amusing episode in the saga of the Somalian pirate infestation off the east coast of Africa.

> "Five of the pirates who hijacked a Saudi supertanker drowned with their share of a $3 million ransom…the day after the bundle of cash was apparently dropped by parachute onto the deck of the ship….The drowned pirates' boat overturned in rough seas….Abukar Haji, uncle of one of the dead pirates, blamed the naval surveillance for the accident that killed his pirate nephew Saturday."

> "'The boat the pirates were traveling in capsized because it was running at high speed because the pirates were afraid of an attack from the warships patrolling around.'"*

The late pirates needn't have worried that any one of the American, French, German, British, Indian, or Chinese naval vessels patrolling the area would attack them. The naval coalition's ineffectual gunboat diplomacy hasn't made a dent in the scale of piracy in the region. The standing order forbids those vessels from firing on pirate boats unless fired upon by the pirates — and what pirate would be crazy enough to fire on a warship that could blow his dingy or speedboat to smithereens? The article reports that pirates attacked over 100 ships last year and that hundreds of sailors remain hostages. Pirates collected over $30 million in ransoms in 2008, a testament to the moral impracticality of the coalition's multinational policy.

No government today is going to instruct its navy to reduce the pirates' hideouts and bases of operation along Somalia's coastline to rubble and floating debris, because no government is going to risk calls for an immediate ceasefire by the United Nations and negotiations. If it ignores such calls, and presses on with the legitimate goal of exterminating an aggressor or a gang of thugs, it would immediately be labeled the brutal aggressor or insensitive villain. Incredibly, that is exactly what has happened as a result of Israel's retaliation against Hamas in Gaza. Hamas and the pirates are seen as the "underdogs." But not all "underdogs" are noble; in history, many of them deserved to be extinguished.

However, to Uncle Abukar, piracy is a legitimate career choice which shouldn't be put in jeopardy by the threat of retaliatory force, as well as to the author of the AP article, Mohamed Olad Hassan, who penned this revealing observation:

"Piracy is one of the few ways to make money in Somalia."

"Make money"? Extortion is a form of theft, and coupled with armed robbery and kidnapping on the high seas, one has a description of piracy. "Making money" is a description of productive, wealth-creating work. But Uncle Abukar and Mr. Hassan exhibit the same grasp of the economics and morality of looters as that of the pirates, outgoing president George W. Bush, president-elect Barack Obama, and Congress. The extortionate, unmitigated looting of the private sector of the economy by Secretary of the Treasury Henry Paulsen and his ilk in Congress and the White House in the so-called "bailout" differs from the Somalian pirates' looting only in scale. The pirates "made" $30 million. The federal government has "made" trillions and stands to "make" trillions more if Obama pushes his "stimulus" program of public works and subsidies through Congress.

The government can "make" money only by stealing it. Like the pirates, it can "make" that money only by employing physical force or the threat of it. It can steal it directly with coercive tax collection, or indirectly through inflation. In the next administration, we will experience large doses of both methods.

President-elect Barack Obama, when he takes the oath of office on January 20th, will swear to protect the United States and uphold the Constitution. But as he made clear throughout his campaign, and has made clear in a number of television interviews and at press conferences since winning the election, he promises to do no such thing. Instead, he has promised to continue the federal government's policy of "saving" the country by looting the productive private sector of wealth and manpower in a program that will make his hero, Franklin D. Roosevelt, look like a rank amateur. He will, with Congress's help, add over a trillion dollars to the over trillion dollars rung up by the Bush administration. Hypothetically, this represents a mortgage on the lives of two or three unborn generations. Hypothetically, because the economy and the country will collapse long before our elective oligarchy and its bureaucratic minions present impoverished Americans with the tax bill.

The point here is deviously simple: The statist economics of Obama, his fiscal appointees, Bush, and virtually every government economist is no more advanced or "sophisticated" than that of the Somalia pirates, or of the cargo cultists of the South Pacific. Wealth exists. It came into existence somehow — *somehow*, because Obama and fellow politicians and bureaucrats, being career public "servants," do not have a first-hand acquaintance with productive work. Wealth, savings, plans, futures, investments all can be magically taken from one person and given to another (redistributed), and a moral end will have been achieved. And when all the wealth, savings, plans, futures and investments have been consumed by the non-producing parasites, and all the new environmental and tax policies have made it impossible for producers to replace them, what then? Neither Obama nor his fiscal appointees can think that far in advance. What is *unthinkable* to them is that the government is the cause of whatever economic crisis they wish to solve. *Intentions*, not facts, govern their statements and actions.

What of those who have been robbed or ruined by such intentions? It is Obama's explicit policy that they should endure their involuntary sacrifices as a matter of duty and in the name of "change." As he told George Stephanopoulos on ABC last Sunday: "Everybody is going to have to give, everybody is going to have to have some skin in the game."

This is gangster talk. Yet our slobbering, fawning news media accepts it and the facetious thinking behind it with wide-eyed rapture. Even when this *faux-naif* back-pedals on his promises, the news media glosses over it with forgiveness or ignorance. When he hedges on an issue, they grin in expectation of some wonderful surprise he has in store. Obama won't need a Department of Disinformation or an Orwellian Ministry of Truth to propagate his economic illiteracy and deceptions. He has the worshipping news media in his pocket willing to wait on his every word.

Well, Adolf Hitler said the same thing when he nationalized Germany's economy in much the same fashion that Bush has nationalized America's. Bush is to Herbert Hoover as Obama is to FDR. Hoover attempted to save "free enterprise" by regulating it, subsidizing failed industries and businesses, and erecting tariff walls to "encourage" it. Every president since then has attempted to "fine tune" or "manage" the economy, discounting or ignoring the element of volition in men when they make choices. Some liberal and conservative pundits claim that Bush abandoned his "free market" principles when he pressured Congress to approve the "bailout" of the auto industry, oblivious to the fact that Bush professed no such principles.

Another clue to Obama's intentions is the character of his cabinet and staff, and the character of his appointees to it. To Obama, it is a "dream team"; for anyone who has wealth to confiscate or freedom to abridge, it is a nightmarish wrecking crew. The cabinet is about as far-left as was Saul Alinsky, the real life Ellsworth Toohey (the collectivist villain in Ayn Rand's *The Fountainhead*) who propounded "community activism" and whose doctrines and methods Obama swallowed whole.

There is Larry Summers, nominated to be head of Obama's National Economic Council, and whose redistributionist philosophy is as primitive as a Somalian pirate's.

There is Timothy Geithner, currently head of the New York Federal Reserve, and nominated to be Secretary of the Treasury, who has confessed ignorance of why companies fail (his mantra: Don't blame government interventionist policies, we had nothing to do with it!). It is not so ironic that he will also be boss of the Internal Revenue Service, and that at his confirmation hearings it was revealed that he failed to file tax returns for several years. He said he was "sorry," and the Senate let him off the hook. For the average taxpayer, however, being "sorry" or having made an "honest mistake" is never good enough to the IRS. But then, Congress is now just Obama's extended Chicago corruption "machine."

There is Rahm Emanuel, the new chief of staff, who has all the charisma and charm of Frank Nitti, Al Capone's "Enforcer" and who is a career power-luster (and enemy of the Second Amendment). He will be in charge of ensuring that all of Obama's cabinet and staff stay in line, and in particular that none of them has ever owned or even touched a gun. After all, Obama wants to make sure that no one can fight or talk back, inside or outside of the White House. As the magazine *America's First Freedom* reported in January:

> "*Time* magazine noted Emanuel's reputation as a 'profane, hyperactive attack dog.' His tactics and style are fully consistent with the world of Chicago machine politics, from which he and Obama sprung."

One can imagine that Emanuel will equip his office with a baseball bat.

There is Eric Holder, Obama's choice for Attorney General, who assured listeners at a convention of the American Constitution Society last summer that Obama would win the election and that the U.S. would then be "run by progressives" — that is, by socialists. Or, by national socialists, if you will.

The American Constitution Society is a left-wing organization founded to counter the influence of The Federalist Society, and its goal is to turn the absolute principles of the Constitution into positivist mush. That is, the Constitution can be whatever the collectivist of the moment wishes it to be. Holder, according to a *Front Page Magazine* article of December 18, was a member of the ACS Board of Advisors. *Front Page* cites a *New York Times* article of December 11 which observed that Holder and the Obama team "will turn to ACS members to fill subcabinet positions and judgeships."

The balance of Obama's designated cabinet and appointees is comprised of recycled Clinton-era officeholders or new unknowns who will work with him and Congress to legislate socialized medicine, radical environmentalism, volunteerism (e.g., his promise of a $4,000 college tuition "credit" to high school and college students who perform 100 hours a year of community service), and in creating new pork barrel jobs to "repair the infrastructure." Shades of the Civilian Conservation Corps. Obama pledged during the campaign to fight Congressional earmarks. What the news media hasn't realized — or perhaps doesn't want to know, because that would put a brake on the giddiness — is that his whole domestic program is one mammoth earmark.

As for Obama's foreign policy, his choice of Hillary Clinton to be Secretary of State, that says it all. Doubtless she will strive to top Condoleezza Rice's pragmatist foreign policy.

It is in the cards that his proposed economic policies will bankrupt the nation and lead to economic havoc. That will be the signal to call for totalitarian measures to bring "discipline" to the anarchy. One can predict with certainty that Obama's speedboat of controls, spending and nascent fascism will capsize in the rough seas of reality, and take its occupants and their ransom money with it. And a good portion of the country.

And then perhaps enough non-docile Americans will learn the hard way and agree with Ayn Rand that a welfare state will always lead to totalitarianism, and decide to do something about it.

January 2009

OCCUPY WALL STREET

The Storm Troopers of OWS

It would be interesting to draw some parallels between Occupy Wall Street and a phenomenon that preceded and that fed the rise of Nazism and the ascension of Nazi power in Germany. That phenomenon was the post-World War I paramilitary Free Corps (*Freikorps*), or *Freebooters.*

When Germany lost the war, its army was disbanded, setting loose hundreds of thousands of German soldiers into a stagnant, debt-ridden, and government controlled economy that had yet to begin paying the Versailles Treaty-mandated reparations that came to billions of dollars. Armies of Free Corps roamed the country, fighting pitched battles with the Communists. They probably decided the outcome of the German Revolution of 1918-1919. The common enemy of the Free Corps was the Communist Party.

However, before the Weimar Republic was formed – and even after it had been installed – Germany was ruled by anarchy, with armed mobs of Free Corps and Communists clashing in city streets, with casualties in the thousands.

In early 1919 the strength of the *Reichswehr*, the regular army, was estimated at 350,000. There were in addition more than 250,000 men enlisted in the various Free Corps. Under the terms of the Versailles Treaty, Germany was required to reduce its armed forces to a maximum of 100,000. Free Corps units were therefore expected to be disbanded.

The parallels discussed here are not the social or even military ones, but the moral ones.

After World War I, the German Army was restricted to 100,000 men, so there were a great amount of soldiers suddenly de-mobilized. Many of these men were hardened into a *Frontgemeinschaft*, a front-line community. It was a spirit of camaraderie that was formed due to the length and horrors of trench warfare of WWI. These paramilitary groups filled a need for many of these soldiers who suddenly lost their "family"—the army. Many of those soldiers were filled with angst, *anger and frustration over the loss and horror* of the war. (Italics mine.)

What have we here? One could say that the protesters of Occupy Wall Street (OWS) have been addled by the "length and horrors" of, well, making a living. By having to earn their own keep. By dealing with a welfare state which they approve of but which they claim isn't generous enough with other people's money. Of being fed up with a Congress that doesn't respond *immediately* to their "needs." By being congenitally outraged by the alleged "pro-business" corruption and lobbying in Congress (but not too outraged by the Solyndra scandal, because that kind of taxpayer fraud and malfeasance is okay with them, it only hurts taxpayers, and it was for a "good cause" – all lobbying and cronyism forgiven). They are unfairly burdened by student loan debt (funded by taxpayers), personal lifestyle debt, and other annoyances.

The irresponsible, the indebted, the reckless, the hankerers after the unearned – that is their "family."

So, there they are, brimming to their eyebrows with "angst, anger, and frustration." Many of them are now infested with diseases and illnesses that soldiers during WWI actually contracted in those trenches. The OWsers complain about the police using pepper spray and using force (having to compel a protester to have his wrists restrained with plastic cuffs). Would they like to experience a dose of mustard gas, instead? How about having one's body riddled by machine gun fire, or being blown to a dozen pieces by an artillery shell? Or being bayoneted? Of simply expiring in water-logged trenches from pneumonia or rickets or typhus? Or dying neglected in a body-strewn, crater-dotted landscape of No Man's Land because medics couldn't get to them for fear of being blown to bits, as well.

No, the OWSers have no taste for that kind of misery. Their misery has no antidote, no cure, no magic pill that would make the "pain" and "anger" go away except the expansion of government powers. Theirs is the pain of the unearned uncollected, the frustration of the entitled who cannot be satiated except by the slavery of those who must provide or subsidize the entitlement.

Occupy Wall Street was no spontaneous phenomenon, but a planned and organized instance of "community organizing," on a scale that would make Saul Alinsky proud. It is orchestrated anarchy intended to cripple the "system," careening towards whatever target its mobs reach a consensus to freeze, personalize, isolate, and polarize, angling for "confrontation" with the police that would put them in the role of "victims of violence" – when they are the initiators of force. One OWS chant is, "The whole world is watching." Unfortunately for the chanters, what the world is watching is a farce, of the police not obliging the trespassers and profanities and noise by cracking skulls and water hosing the hordes. Which is what ought to have happened the first time OWS blocked a street or broke a window.

(Interesting side-note: secular leftists do not have a monopoly on Alinsky's "Rules for Radicals." Islamist outfits like the Council on American-Islamic Relations, The Islamic Circle, and other Muslim "advocacy" groups already practice targeting and personalizing issues, and with growing success. They are masters of those rules.)

"Occupying" a public space and blocking its use by the public, however, is an initiation of force. Zuccotti Park in New York, for example, is a nominally private park open to the public. OWS closed it to all but its own. The whole world was watching while the filth accumulated in that park, while crimes like rape and theft and threatening local businesses occurred, while a "flying squad" of pillagers went on a rampage in Oakland, while hundreds have been arrested with kid-gloves and led away to school buses. One strongly suspects that what OWS was plotting and hoping for was a repeat of the violence of the 1968 Democratic Convention in Chicago. The news media were on the side of the left even back then. But, it hasn't happened – not yet. It doesn't even have a Tom Hayden to excuse, explain, and sanction their cause and its violence. On the surface, OWS has a central nervous system but no brain, no guiding agenda or petition of grievances except a desire to destroy and loot the ruins.

Also, on the surface, OWS does not resemble the pre-Nazi Free Corps. The rabble sports no uniforms, no semblance of military or other discipline, no decorum to speak of, no homogeneity of any kind except for the ubiquitous slovenliness of appearance and mind. It is a conglomeration of slobs, wannabe criminals, punks, weirdos, women with bees in their bonnets and men with only half a deck of cards in their craniums. The variety of protest signs, usually scrawled on cardboard, and often revealing a profound illiteracy in spelling and grammar, testify to the unity of "angst and anger" and the triumph of a university education. OWS brandishes a variety of banners, including the American, but the Palestinian and Puerto Rican flags were also in evidence. On the whole, what OWS is rebelling against is reality, a reality their elective ilk have created.

But like the Free Corps, OWS is a kind of syndicate or an uneasy alliance of disparate collectivist causes and organizations. Some Free Corps upheld the

Weimer Republic. Others fought to bring it down. OWS is an amalgam of communists, welfare state liberals, old school radicals, gray panther leftists, new age hippies, holders of worthless degrees, the professionally unemployed, the perpetually alienated, the clinically certifiably disgruntled, career vagrants, vehicles of middle class guilt, black power advocates, Muslims, anti-Semites, Hispanics of indeterminate national origin, unions, AmeriCorps manqués, Peace Corps veterans, environmentalists – all the bilious movements that mushroomed on the mulch of American educational philosophy, and that were prepared and sanctioned by grade and high schools and universities and patronized, idolized, and encouraged by the news media.

But while Barack Obama is blamed for OWS and its violence and health issues and the whole mess, it would be unfair to lay it all on his doorstep. Obama and OWS, like Tom Hayden and the radicals of the 1960's and 1970's, are a consequence of the collapse of philosophy and the disparagement of reason. OWS is merely the post-Woodstock, second wave of Borg raiders with bachelor's degrees.

The protesters of OWS are prime cannon fodder, and perfect recruits for an American version of the Free Corps. We have seen how quickly they can be called up for "action"; that mobs of "Occupiers" sprang up almost simultaneously in cities all over the country testifies to the availability of so many aimless foot soldiers and to a committee or cabal of planners and "community organizers" working behind the scenes and who remain undiscovered and undiscussed by the news media. As we get further into the presidential election campaign, we will see more of this kind of "action." The "interruption" of Michelle Bachmann's speech in South Carolina by OWS, and the attempted storming of the Americans for Prosperity event in Washington DC, are but a taste of what is ahead – unless the planners decide that OWS has been a failure, even for the dereliction of responsibility of various municipal leaders of having let the movement grow out of control, as Mayor Bloomberg did in New York. He had Zuccotti Park cleared out – and then invited OWS back, *sans* tents, tarps, and other camping gear. As though that would make a difference.

The denizens of OWS can be organized into roaming and violent Free Corps. They can be taught discipline and minimal decorum. The SEIU, the UAW, and other strong-arm outfits can give them advice on logistics, manpower, and offer seminars on the art of news-hogging police provocation. They can be given any cause their philosopher-kings wish to give them, and most OWSers will be amenable to it. The news media will give the new Free Corps their blessing, and cheer them on from their insulated TV studios and round tables, and call it freedom of speech, when in fact OWS is an enemy of the First Amendment.

85

As with the German Free Corps and the consolidation of power that brooks no rivalry – the Free Corps SA was purged, while the Free Corps SS was elevated – there will be purges from OWS and a campaign to paint it in respectable colors. The purges won't be pretty; there will be weeping and wailing and the gnashing of teeth. As with the non-violent Tea Party movement, it will seek to become an influential "voice" in Washington (not that it lacks such a voice now, as witness the endorsement of OWS by the POTUS, Nancy Pelosi, Harry Reid, and other America-changing activists).

OWS in this instance is merely an exploratory phenomenon, to see what will or will not be tolerated, of feeling out the "establishment" for weaknesses and sizing up its strengths. As of this writing, the "establishment" has no proven strengths to counter the intended terrorism of OWS but its own inertia. It has no philosophy of individual rights, of laissez-faire, of limited government, of an understanding of the purpose of government. Fundamentally, in the deepest sense, the federal, state, and municipal governments are one with OWS.

2012 will be a watershed election year. Chickens came home to roost in 1968. In 2012, it will be vultures who flock in large numbers to pick at the carcass of the American Republic.

November 2011

Occupy Wall Street: An Axis of Enemies

A number of stark contrasts should be noted between the freedom of speech and assembly as practiced by Occupy Wall Street and Pamela Geller.

On the one hand, Occupy Wall Street (OWS) has literally taken over a piece of public property near Wall Street in New York City by force of its protesters and with the tacit sanction of the city and its mayor, Michael Bloomberg. OWS has made itself not only a public nuisance, but an unsanitary and dangerous one.

OWS has attracted every collectivist, socialist, communist, environmental, and even anti-Semitic loon to its cause. It is a grab-bag of "movements," ranging from the call for the "reform" of Wall Street (meaning its abolition) and the persecution of Jews. If you are "anti-establishment" and have a gripe against "the system" – whether you are a Wal-Mart employee, an unemployed, a welfare recipient, a trust fund tyke, unsure of or unhappy with your gender, a pal of the Palestinians, an indebted career student, a Facebook socialist, a son or daughter of Woodstock, a public employee, an SEIU or UAW thug, an "artist," "writer," or "musician," a fan of Farrakhan, a New or Old Black Panther, a Jew against Israel, a Muslim against Jews, an anarchist, a neo-Nazi, a Marxist, a Trotskyite, or something in between – OWS is the place to go and be.

The Sugar Land Tea Party reserved a conference room at the Hyatt Place Houston/Sugar Land Hotel to hear Pamela Geller, prominent anti-jihadist and anti-Sharia advocate, speak last week on the subject of the dangers of stealth Sharia and stealth jihad in the United States. The Hyatt abruptly, with little or no notice, cancelled the event, originally citing "security reasons." The Sugar Land Tea Party rushed to find another venue for the event, a community center. What security reasons did the hotel name? "Complaints" by Muslims that Geller's explanation of Sharia law constituted "hate speech."

The Mainstream Media (MSM) has drooled over, cooed about, and coddled OWS, providing it with free publicity it could never afford to pay for itself and implicitly approving of its multitudinous aims. It is tantamount to inveighing against prostitution, but demonizing the "johns" and painting the prostitutes as "victims of the system." The Corporation for Public Broadcasting (aka Communist Public Brainwashing, "funded by viewers and taxpayers like you") through its outlets of NPR and PBS is standing in the corner, treating OWS "neutrally" as though it were a volcanic eruption or an outbreak of salmonella, but not questioning the legitimacy of the protest.

All one hears from OWS, however, is "hate speech" directed against the rich, against corporations, against Jews, against capitalism, against freedom. This is "hate speech" approved by the MSM, while anyone who criticizes Islam, Sharia law, or anything remotely Arabic is branded an "Islamophobe" or a "racist."

Some protesters, apparently, are more equal than others. This is how things are done and said on America's own *Animal Farm*, a leftist fantasy park that exists only in the minds of the MSM. Of course, career filthy-rich left-wing propagandist filmmaker Michael Moore ("Jabber the Hutt") and intellectual dwarves like actress Susan Saranden weighed in with their thumbs up for OWS. Right. Revolution now! But don't touch *my* stuff!

Had Geller a right to object to the Hyatt cancelling the venue of her talk? Did the Hyatt's action constitute suppression of speech? Did it violate her right to speak?

Nominally, the Hyatt exercised its right to cancel the venue, because the hotel is private property. If someone or some organization uses another's private property as a "soapbox" to promulgate specific views, it is with the tacit or express permission of the property owner. But Geller was not going to address her audience about the wisdom of buying gold stocks, life insurance, or new computer technology. Nothing as mundane as that. She was going to speak on the perils, inequities, and insidiousness of Sharia. This is an ideological subject, not a "practical" one. The Hyatt may have been indifferent to the subject. It is reflective of the "What? Me Worry?" attitude most American business executives exhibit when confronted with important moral and ideological issues.

That indifference ended when the local chapter of the Council on American-Islamic Relations mounted a telephone protest against the event, causing Hyatt to think twice and withdraw the venue. Hyatt executives then became "worried." In concrete terms, the Hyatt did not violate Geller's First Amendment rights. But seen in a broader context, Hyatt's action *contributed* not only to the suppression of her freedom of speech by CAIR and its fellow Hamas- and Muslim Brotherhood-spawned organizations – *dhimmis* make such useful, facilitating proxies – but of its own, and in doing so advanced the agenda of Islamists to gut the First Amendment guarantee in order to protect itself from legitimate criticism and exposure.

Such is the stuff American businessmen are made of today. Can you imagine what would *not* have happened had the colonials who gathered on Lexington Green, upon only hearing the distant tramp and cadence drums of approaching British regulars, said among themselves: "Uh, do we really want to do this? I mean, they can bomb our homes, harass our customers, make life miserable for us if we stand here. They got us out-gunned anyway. What's the point? We got crops to tend to. I'm out of here."

OWS, on the other hand, not only does not face the kind of obstacle and censure that Geller, Robert Spencer, and other writers about Islamic jihad and Sharia, but has been given a free hand by the MSM and various municipal governments, and without recrimination, retribution, or rebuttal, to slander, libel, trash, and spit on all the hands that feed its yelping, chanting, non-

producing, parasitical minions, and make their sorry lives possible –
corporations, investors, innovators, taxpayers, and even government.
Is the hand of President Barack Obama to be seen in OWS and the Hyatt back-
down? One cannot but help suspect that the answer is *Yes*. Here are some
interesting threads.

Obama "sympathizes" with OWS. He is on "their side." This is his
kind of "community action." It follows the prescribed methodology and tactics
of Saul Alinsky Rule No. 13 to bring about "change" or "reform": Identify,
isolate, freeze and escalate.

> "I think it expresses the frustrations that the American people feel," he
> said Thursday. "People are frustrated and the protesters are giving
> voice to a more broad-based frustration about how our financial
> system works." (NBC)

This is Alinsky-lingo dressed in the pinafore of political
verisimilitude.

> "The most important thing we can do right now is those of us in
> leadership letting people know that we understand their struggles and
> we are on their side, and that we want to set up a system in which hard
> work, responsibility, doing what you're supposed to do, is rewarded,"
> Obama tells ABC News.. "And that people who are irresponsible, who
> are reckless, who don't feel a sense of obligation to their communities
> and their companies and their workers that those folks aren't
> rewarded." (Weekly Standard)

Obama tried to equate the anti-big-government sentiments and civil
behavior of the Tea Party rallies and town halls with Occupy Wall Street. It is
his version of the Bronx Cheer:

> The president also compares the protesters to the Tea Party. "In some
> ways, they're not that different from some of the protests that we saw
> coming from the Tea Party," Obama says. "Both on the left and the
> right, I think people feel separated from their government. They feel
> that their institutions aren't looking out for them." (Weekly Standard)

Frankly, the government isn't separated enough from Americans.
There is hardly a realm of action in which the government does not set the
terms or make life more expensive and complicated. Americans who value
their freedom do not want their government looking out for them, except to
protect their individual rights. They want to be left alone, not nurtured,
regulated, and throttled from cradle to grave.

It is the rabble of OWS who wish to be wards of the government. Read their signs. Listen to their chants. Observe their behavior.

So, even if the Democratic National Committee actually has had no hand in the fomenting and growth of OWS, a sanction from the highest office in the land is culpability enough.

It should not be surprising that Islamist supremacists wish to share the stage with socialist supremacists. In too many photos of OWS in New York and of "occupations" in cities around the country can be seen men wearing Yasser Arafat-inspired keffiyah around their necks. These photos predated news of an Islamic sanction of OWS. Their presence among the rabble also comports with OWS signs that call for the end of the "occupation" of Gaza. Do we detect a smidgen of double-standards here, concerning "occupations"? Yes, but don't tax an OWS protester with it. These people wouldn't know a double standard if it bit them in their butts.

It is only a matter of time that we will see photos of neo-Nazis marching, chanting, singing, sign-waving, harassing, defecating, urinating, shoulder-to-shoulder with Islamist supremacists, flaunting their neo-Nazi swastika banners. Think that's impossible? Think again. Rocky Suhayda, head of the American Nazi Party, assured his members it was okay to join OWS, even though there are "non-whites" taking part in OWS:

> In a message posted Thursday on its official website, organization head Rocky Suhayda said members of the "pro-white" movement should join and support the Occupy demonstrators because they share a common enemy: The "Judeo-capitalist banksters."

> Suhayda said though many "racialists" are concerned about the demonstrations because the "many protesters are non-white and/or 'communists,'" that shouldn't matter because they are all against the same "evil, corrupted, degenerate capitalist elitists."

> "… Even Adolf Hitler's NSDAP had to vote with open communists on some issues to achieve their goals. WE need to utilize and support every movement of dissent against this evil American empire, regardless of which end of the political spectrum it originates from."

Most people do not know that Hitler also stooped to dealing with those "racially degenerate" Arabs (who were as bad as or worse than those Jewish-led communists!) when it came to eradicating Jews. He had a close relationship with the Grand Mufti of Jerusalem and planned with him a Mideast version of the Holocaust.

Now, the Hyatt Hotel chain is owned or controlled by Penny Pritzker. Geller mentions her in her article about Hyatt's dhimmitude. Pritzker is another billionaire on the Obama bus. She was his national campaign finance manager in 2008. She oversaw the Superior Bank subprime mortgage scandal. She was recruited to donate money to Obama's campaigns. She is still active for Obama, serving on a committee to raise (more) money for his 2012 reelection campaign.

President Obama's close relationship with Warren Buffett goes back to his Illinois Senate run; now the billionaire investor is helping Obama not only on the tax fairness front, but in fund-raising for his 2012 re-election bid. Buffett hits Chicago Oct. 27 for a $35,800-per person dinner and reception. The host committee includes Obama's major Chicago based finance team: Jim Crown, Vicki & Bruce Heyman, Mellody Hobson Steve Koch, Penny Pritzker, John Rogers Jr., David Scherer.

Who are all those people? Rich people. But the kind of "1%" rich people OWS studiously neglects to excoriate or curse. But, don't bother pointing out the contradiction to the protesters. Contradictions are beyond their grasp, excised from their minds by "reformist" educators in public schools and in the universities.

My betting is that Pritzker ordered the Houston Hyatt executives to scratch Geller's event. Word got to her, she was appalled ("I won't allow hate speech to be spewed on *my* properties!"), or was warned, or was advised, and out went the order.

Occupy Wall Street is an in-plain-sight, transparent vortex of every collectivist and totalitarian cause and movement that ever befouled American soil and that ever assaulted American liberties. "Soaking the rich," ending property rights, collectivizing or nationalizing all property, can only lead to across-the-board censorship, the end of freedom of speech, and the scuttling of the First Amendment. There would be no private property left on which to advocate or oppose anything. Pamela Geller insists on exercising her freedom of speech. Occupy Wall Street and all its enablers, supporters, allies, and financiers insist on ending it.

That is "Polarization" with a capital *P.* Anyone with an ounce of self-respect and who values his life, liberty, property, and pursuit of happiness, should be for it. After all, there is no "coming together," no reconciliation, no "common ground" possible with OWS or Sharia law. They are both the mortal enemies of America.

October 2011

Occupy Wall Street's Declaration of Dependence

If the unwashed and odiferous masses of Occupy Wall Street – that less than one percent of the American population, most of whom are at work and do not have the free time to camp out in public or private parks – originally gathered to protest a grab-bag of disparate, alleged and imagined offenses, they are now getting direction from the undead of the Left. Occupy Wall Street (OWS) is being given guidance by those who know what they want. *Power.*

The election of Barack Obama in 2008, together with a single term in the White House, with good luck and good premises, may be looked back upon as the Last Hurrah of the Left in this country. Obama literally campaigned on his own "occupy" mantra: OWH. Which he did, and trashed it, too. The Left has been the ideological vessel of socialism and tyranny. It fooled no one, not even its exponents. It had been found out, exposed, and repudiated, more by the failure of People's Republics worldwide, including the Soviet Union, which ran out of economic steam, and Red China, which retained the trappings of Communism but turned fascist, than by any argument offered by the Right. Reality repudiated Communism and every other form of collectivism.

The allegedly unemployed of OWS have it all wrong: the economy is not fascist, Wall Street is not by nature fascist, and a chief problem with today's economy is that the government is in it. OWS wants it to take over the economy. Which would mean the end of the economy.

If they want a taste of genuine fascism, they ought to apply for a job in China. There they would get a taste of "crony capitalism" but wouldn't be allowed to "occupy" Tiananmen Square to protest it. Not after what happened there the last time, when genuine freedom-fighters were brutally dispersed, maimed or killed by tanks, and rounded up and imprisoned for life. The heroes of Tiananmen Square erected a Statue of Liberty as their symbol of defiance.

The OWS adopts a percentile in a vague silhouette of George Washington as a claim on the wealthy and on anyone else who earns more than $20,000 a year.

Obama gave the Left's dead battery a jump-start. Until the current administration, the Left as a motivational force was dying a deserved death. Now the redistributive clunker is merely sputtering, coughing, dying and reviving, trying to stay alive. Its ideological carburetor is unequal to the task of reconciling the air of its ideology with the gasoline of reality, and must be struck repeatedly with a two-by-four to get it working again. Its spark plugs fire haphazardly, and half of them are dead. Its tires are bald. Its transmission needs rebuilding.

The Tea Party movement called the administration's and Congress's policies for what they were and continue to be: political and economic clunkers, unsafe at any speed and liable to die anytime, anywhere. If it moves at all, it is only because there are a pair of donkeys in harness, disguised as politicians. Obama and Congress still insist that the clunker is salvageable and that Americans pour more and more money into it to keep it running.

Cash for Clunkers? Remember that Obama-inspired scam? The catch now is that you give Congress and all the federal bureaucracies the cash, not the other way around. There's not even a figment of a trade involved. Just expropriation, regulation, and tyranny.
This is a clunker that should be sitting on cinder blocks in Arkansas, right next to the Clinton Presidential Library in Little Rock, with a bronze plaque affixed to its rusted bumper: HERE LIES WELFARE STATISM. GOOD RIDDANCE.

OWS wishes Congress or the government to give everyone cash as an entitlement, or at least a guaranteed job. Where is the money to come from? The Bureau of Printing and Engraving. To pay for what? Whatever the members of OWS wish to have – provided they can find it to buy, for if they get their way, there won't be much left on store shelves to buy. All those evil corporations will have perished or been nationalized.

OWS can be taken as not so much a Last Hurrah as an inarticulate, spittle-spewing, obscene gesture to everything its denizens hold malice for. The "99% Declaration" is an *à la carte* prescription for socialist rule. "Democratically" adopted and enforced, it would be the end of "democracy," or rule by "the people." It would pave the way for a French Revolution-style directorate of dictators in which "the people" have no say.

This in turn would pave the way for a man on a white horse. Or a palomino pony. Or on another unicorn.

Section IV of the "99% Declaration" contains twenty clauses that call for a complete takeover of the economy. The first three abolish the First Amendment vis-à-vis election campaigns.

1. Elimination of the Corporate State. *Implementing an immediate ban on all private contributions of money and gifts, to all politicians in federal office,* *from individuals, corporations, "political action committees," "super political action committees," lobbyists, unions and all other private sources of money or thing of value to be replaced by the fair, equal and total public financing of all federal political campaigns. We categorically REJECT the concepts that corporations are persons or that money is equal to free speech because if that were so, then only the wealthiest people and corporations would have a voice.*

And what happened in November, 2008? Was or was not Barack Obama, who sympathizes with OWS, elected by these same people? Did or did he not have the help of the Mainstream Media? Did or did not major corporations and wealthy individuals contribute millions to his campaign chest? Are they still not donating? And, since when was money ever equal to free speech? Is this is just a sloppy metaphor? If all federal political campaigns were to be totally and exclusively "publicly financed," by what measure would a federal election committee determine who was qualified to run for office, and who was not, whose petition of signatures was acceptable, and whose was not? And if only corporations and the wealthiest have had a voice in politics, why is the country sliding perilously close to complete socialism, in which they would be nationalized, eliminated, imprisoned, or shot out of hand?
There is no such thing as a "corporate state." All that exists now is an omnivorous federal government determined to absorb everything.

2. **Rejection of the Citizens United Case**. *The immediate abrogation, even if it requires a Constitutional Amendment, of the outrageous and anti-democratic holding in the "Citizens United" case proclaimed by the United States Supreme Court. This heinous decision equates the payment of money by corporations, wealthy individuals and unions to politicians with the exercise of protected free speech. We, the People, demand that this institutional bribery and corruption never again be deemed protected free speech.*
It does no such thing as "equating."

The *Citizens United* case is a special bugbear of OWS, but we should never expect the lights of OWS to examine anything closely enough to get at the truth. Hans A. von Spakovsky, in his article, "The Occupy Wall Streeters – Destroying the First Amendment," clarifies this issue:

The claim that the *Citizens United* decision allows payment of "money by corporations" and unions to politicians is a myth that liberals and campaign reformers continue to spew. Corporations and unions are prohibited from making campaign contributions to politicians by federal law, and that law has *not* been overturned by the Supreme Court (although some would argue that it should be overturned by Congress).

Citizens United held that the First Amendment prohibits Congress from censoring the political speech of any entity, and that includes independent expenditures that fund political speech. That decision is in the greatest traditions of liberty and free speech, the most fundamental principles upon which this country was founded.

Furthermore, apparently OWS cannot imagine the prospect of any politician or any advocacy group spending millions to broadcast or publicize its issues, and an individual *not* being convinced or persuaded on any specific issue. In fact, Obama spent millions on his election campaign, but I was not convinced, persuaded, or even duped by his rhetoric. Quite the opposite.

3. **Elimination of Private Contributions to Politicians.** *Prohibiting all federal public employees, officers, officials or their immediate family members from ever being employed by any corporation, individual or business that they specifically regulated while in office; nor may any public employee, officer, official or their immediate family members own or hold any stock or shares in any corporation they regulated while in office until a full 5 years after their term is completed; a complete lifetime ban on the acceptance of all gifts, services, money or thing of value, directly or indirectly, by any elected or appointed federal official or their immediate family members, from any person, corporation, union or other entity that the public official was charged to specifically regulate while in office. In sum, elected politicians and public employees in regulatory roles may only collect their salary, generous healthcare benefits and pension. Any person, including corporate employees, found guilty and convicted of violating these rules in a court of law by proof beyond a reasonable doubt, shall be sentenced to a term of mandatory imprisonment of no less than one year and not more than ten years.*

I have a much, much simpler proposal: get the government out of the economy. This means forbidding the government to fund anything but national defense and the courts and the bare minimum expenses of operating Congress. Abolish all subsidies to private enterprises and companies. Abolish most of the Cabinet, especially the Departments of Education, Energy, Agriculture, Commerce, Interior, Labor, Health and Human Services, Housing and Urban Development, and Transportation. None of these offices and attendant bureaucracies has any legitimate purpose in a limited government. Keep the Copyright and Patent offices; they perform legitimate, rights-protecting functions. Abolish all civil service unions. Abolish 99% of the various rights-violating, regulatory bureaucracies.

Abolish House and Senate salaries and all special, protected perks and privileges, and pay Senators and Congressmen on a *per diem* basis, for the expenses incurred in getting to Washington to represent their constituencies as briefly as possible; grant them closely audited meal allowances and board at a Super 8 Motel. I'm betting that an argument could even be made against that fillip. The goal of all this abolishing would be to discourage any political ambition but the desire to protect and uphold life, liberty, property and the pursuit of happiness.

The balance of the "99% Declaration" is so predictable as to be dull reading. It cadges other, non-OWS proposals for term limits. It calls for a "fair tax code," as though any tax code is "fair." But from a collectivist's perspective, OWS's "fair tax" seeks to soak the rich and expropriate the wealth of those who are also not in the "1%." It demands health care for all or the adoption of the single-payer system, completely omitting mention of the status of those who are to provide such health care: doctors, surgeons, nurses, and other medical personnel who presumably would be drafted into government service and paid pittance. We all know how that idea was received by doctors. Very few were willing to labor in a "ready reserve."

The Declaration comports with environmentalist ideology by making Mother Earth a party to the proposed national general assembly of OWS. The clause citing a demand for debt reduction, given the amounts of money it would take to bring OWS's fantasy world into existence, is an exercise in *reductio ad absurdum*. Point Nine demands jobs for all Americans. As whose employees? Doing what?

9. **Jobs for All Americans**. *Passage of a comprehensive job and job-training act like the American Jobs Act to employ our citizens in jobs that are available with specialized training and by putting People to work now by repairing America's crumbling infrastructure. We also recommend the establishment of an online international job exchange to match employers with skilled workers or employers willing to train workers in 21st century skills. In conjunction with a new jobs act, reinstitution of the Works Progress Administration and Civilian Conservation Corps or a similar emergency governmental agency tasked with creating new public works projects to provide jobs to the 46 million People living in poverty, the 9.1% unemployed and 10% underemployed.*

In short, make everyone a public employee, dependent on what public service jobs are available in a statist, command economy and on what some bureaucrat or "czar" determines is a livable wage. Private jobs, providing such an economy doesn't first collapse, will be few and hard to find. And regulated.

The Declaration demands universal, across-the-board student loan forgiveness, to be paid for by socking it to Wall Street with a "reparations" surcharge. After all, didn't you know, Wall Street caused the economic collapse of 2007-2008? Well, no, it didn't. It was government meddling in the economy with subprime mortgages and the like.

Displaying their ignorance, the authors of this point forget, if they ever knew, that student loans have been rising for decades with the cost of higher education. And who is funding that rising cost? The federal government, by inflating the currency and causing schools to compete for those extra tuition dollars. With what consequence? Graduates in a variety of specialties and studies that have little or no value in the private sector. Graduates who are barely literate and have no thinking or critical skills, which were beginning to be erased from their minds in grade and high school.

The Declaration demands the immediate passage of the Dream Act. That is, its authors wish the ballot boxes to be stuffed by illegal immigrants who vote early and often.

There are six other "demands" in the Declaration, all worth a critique, but one of the last ones exhibits a special species of ignorance. It demands that the Federal Reserve Bank be ended. Yes, end the Fed. Get the government out of the economy. But, excuse me, your personships, the Fed is not "privately owned." It is a creature of government, and it regulates banks. This ending of the Fed, says the Declaration, should be in conjunction with a moratorium on foreclosures. And mixed in with the demand to abolish the Electoral College – the last safeguard against populist tyranny and the democracy the Founders so feared – it advocates the creation of national identity cards under the ruse of voter registration.

It is nearly laughable that the unwashed masses of OWS are now complaining about crime in Zuccotti Park, and about freeloaders and the certified "homeless" who have found a hassle-free nest, free food, and refuge among its malodorous ranks. After all, OWS advocates freeloading as a right. It is the perfect model for anarchy, complete with ineffective "security" and the Woodstock spirit of free sex, unlimited drugs, noise that passes for music, uncollected garbage, hepatitis, syphilis, bugs, and rats. One wonders how many of these people in the future are going to be crowding into "free clinics" demanding to be cured of whatever maladies they picked up in Zuccotti Park.

All in all, the "99% Declaration" is nothing less than an appeal for dependence on government and an explicit surrender to anyone who lusts for power.

October 2011

CLINTON *REDUX*

Hillary Clinton Auditions for Lady Macbeth

Come, you spirits, that tend on mortal thoughts, unsex me, and fill me from the crown to the toe topful of direst cruelty. (Lady Macbeth, *Macbeth*, Act 1, Scene 5)

Secretary of State Hillary Clinton, a woman scorned, first by her husband former President Bill, who favored swishier skirts and less nagging, and then by the Democrat machine in favor of a nobody from nowhere during the 2008 election, finds every little opportunity to vent her wrath on her own country. Her latest roller-pin is reminiscent of Lady Macbeth's supplications to be given the nerve to commit murder. Hanging out so often with all those Muslim men has more or less unsexed her to the point that she is willing to commit, if not murder, then a dire cruelty which arguably could be defined as treason.

As reported by Jihad Watch and other news outlets, the principle advocates of a move to criminalize the legitimate examination of any religious faith, especially Islam, are globalist One-Worlders who seek to bring the U.S. under their thumb. Their particular "one world" is a global caliphate, with or without United Nations trappings. Their particular bugbear is "Islamophobia" or a legitimate fear of Islam and Sharia law – briefly, of Islamic totalitarianism.

JEDDAH, Ramadan 1/Aug 1 (IINA)-During the next few months, Washington plans to host a coordination meeting to discuss with the Organization of Islamic Cooperation (OIC) how to implement resolution no. 16/18 on combating defamation of religions, and how to prevent stereotypes depicting religions and their followers; as well as disseminating religious tolerance, which has been endorsed by the UN Human Rights Council last March, in agreement with Western countries. The resolution was adopted after lengthy discussions held between the OIC and countries in which the phenomenon of Islamophobia is in [*sic*] the rise.

The U.S. Secretary of State Hillary Clinton had announced the intention of the U.S. State Department to organize a coordination meeting during her participation in the meeting which she co-chaired with the OIC Secretary General, Professor Ekmeleddin Ihsanoglu in Istanbul on 15 July 2011. The meeting issued a joint statement emphasizing the dire need for the implementation of resolution 16/18.

According to informed sources in the Organization of Islamic Cooperation, the two sides, in addition to other European parties, will hold a number of specialized meetings of experts in law and religion in order to finalize the legal aspect on how to better implement the UN resolution.

The OIC recently changed its name to the Organization of Islamic Cooperation (from "Conference"), believing it was less frightening or portentous, and more pacific and amenable.

But "Islamophobes" do not have a monopoly on fear. The distinction between "Islamophobes" and "Freedom-of-Speechophobes" is that the first group does not seek to gag, penalize, suppress, or criminalize speech per se. "Islamophobes" do not fear freedom of speech. They value and encourage it.

For a glimpse of ideal dhimmitude, in which Islam is a protected religion, see this Christiane Amanpour sales pitch on the lifestyle of Aramco employees in Saudi Arabia. Notice the abject deference its American employees pay to Islam and Saudi Arabia. This is a glimpse of one's life under Sharia law, except that you won't be horseback riding and living in a privileged infidel's ghetto. The Americans you see here are dhimmis, and Amanpour approves.

Speechophobes, on the other hand, fear the unfettered, free discussion and criticism of Islam because otherwise Islamophobes might convince others that Islam is a primitive, barbaric, man-hating system ripe for totalitarian implementation, that every facet and aspect of Islam, from its iconic "Prophet" to its magic wand metaphysics to its schizophrenic *Koran* to its damnation of non-believers is open to scrutiny, refutation, and even mockery. Islam begs to be insulted on top of injury, to be defamed, blasphemed, and denigrated.

> The sources said that the upcoming meetings aim at developing a legal basis for the UN Human Rights Council's resolution which help in enacting domestic laws for the countries involved in the issue, as well as formulating international laws preventing inciting hatred resulting from the continued defamation of religions.

> On the other hand, the OIC Secretary General, Ekmeleddin Ihsanoglu, stressed that the crime committed recently in Norway was a result of the rise of the extreme right in Europe and its easy mobility in political circles. He said that the OIC had warned several times against of what might be called institutionalization of the phenomenon of Islamophobia through the involvement of the European extreme right in government institutions and political action....

There is only one religion that has been consistently "defamed," and that is Islam. From the mass murders in the West to the everyday murders and persecutions in Muslim countries, Islam has been the inspiration of ninety-nine-point-nine percent of the atrocities. If it looks like a duck, walks like a duck, and quacks like a duck, then it must be Islam. Can anyone be blamed for identifying the duck? Especially if it leaves a trail of blood and guts behind its waddle?

Clinton did not need to conjure up "spirits" to imbue her with the strength to betray her own country. She sat with them in Jeddah and plotted to bring Islamic censorship to the U.S. via the U.N. She is such a special dhimmi to the Islamists that she apparently has been granted dispensation and need not wear a headscarf in their company or in Saudi Arabia. There are no pictures of her in Saudi Arabia wearing one. Any other woman caught on Saudi Arabian streets without one would be jailed by the religious police, Muslim or non-Muslim.

Clinton's character aside – and that could be the subject of book-length treatment and not a pretty picture – why would she be willing to sell out not only America, but Israel? Because, on a purely diplomatic and "practical" standpoint, she will not challenge, first, the anti-Semitic nature of Islam, and second, the notion that Islam is a "religion of peace" (as Westerners perceive it, not as Muslims know it is not).

Ron Kampeas of Capital J discusses this issue and has this to reveal about the OIC and its agenda for censorship, or the suppression of speech if it "defames" Islam:

In a revealing comment on the nature of this controversy, the observer for Indonesia remarked in the UN Sub-Commission on Prevention of Discrimination and Protection of Minorities (1997, December 22) that "it could only be assumed that the motive of those who insulted Islam was to generate conflict with Islamic peoples or even to justify the injustices to which they were currently being subjected" (para. 14). Accordingly, Indonesia – along with other OIC states – maintains the view that no critical comment concerning Islam is justifiable – regardless of whether the forum is academic or the objective pursued is a worthy one, such as the elimination of discrimination. Underscoring this perspective two years earlier, a representative from Iran informed the UN that "in the opinion [of] the Organization of the Islamic Conference the right to freedom of thought, opinion and expression could in no case justify blasphemy."

So, those who "insult" Islam are responsible for the murders and persecution of not only Muslims in Muslim and non-Muslim countries, but of non-Muslims? (Call it the Oslo-Breivik Syndrome, newly discovered by Islamists.) These are not "injustices"? Stonings, amputations, female genital mutilation, beatings, child rape, woman rape, mandatory self-effacement, ritual self-abnegation, and the whole Islamic culture do not constitute injustice?

To the OIC, and with the silent consent of Hillary Clinton, freedom of thought, opinion and expression do not justify "blaspheming" or "defaming" Islam. Period. And Clinton will help the OIC find legal ways to enforce that censorship in this country. She will "cooperate."

The United States oath of office for the President is specified in the Constitution (Article II, Section 1):

I do solemnly swear (or affirm) that I will support and defend the Constitution of the United States against all enemies, foreign and domestic; that I will bear true faith and allegiance to the same; that I take this obligation freely, without any mental reservation or purpose of evasion; and that I will well and faithfully discharge the duties of the office on which I am about to enter. So help me God.

So help me, Allah? If she had been elected President, would she have simply mouthed the oath of office, as Barack Obama did, and proceeded to *not* preserve, protect and defend this country, as he has done? Would her policies have been any different from Obama's, or worse?

Is she one of the Weird Sisters of *Macbeth*, or the nagging, instigating wife of Macbeth?

102

Whichever she is, it is the task of "Islamophobes" to undo what she has done and will do. We should not expect her to ever wring her hands in regret, as Lady Macbeth did in the end.

We will not suffer the fate of King Duncan. We will not be silenced.

August 2011

Hillary Clinton's Uncle Ellsworth

While truth can often be stranger than fiction, the one can complement the other.

This thought occurred to me when I began to read Hillary Rodham Clinton's 1969 political science thesis, written in "partial fulfillment of the requirements for the Bachelor of Arts degree under the Special Honors Program, Wellesley College, Wellesley, Massachusetts." Its title is: "'There Is Only the Fight...': An Analysis of the Alinsky Model."

Four or five pages into this paper, I was struck by the similarities between the relationships of Ellsworth Toohey and Catherine Halsey in Ayn Rand's novel, *The Fountainhead*, and of Saul D. Alinsky and young Hillary D. Rodham, college student. Copies of this 91-page typewritten paper, interspersed here and there with handwritten corrections, are now circulating all over the Internet, accompanied by commentary that is largely critical and often deprecatory in nature.

Ellsworth Toohey, as readers probably know, is the power-seeking arch villain in Rand's novel, and Catherine Halsey his niece, whose self-esteem he mercilessly attacks at every opportunity and succeeds in destroying, reducing her to a selfless, public service drudge.

Saul David Alinsky (1909-1972) was a real-life "radical" who specialized in organizing "communities" for local political agitation rather than attempting the broader political machinations of Toohey. He was a second-rank power luster – certainly less charismatic than Toohey, to judge by his biography – but his fundamental methodology of acquiring power – not for himself, he always said, but for whomever he deemed the "dispossessed" – is essentially the same as Toohey's, which Rand so brilliantly dramatized in Toohey's character.

This commentary will focus on the parallels between the pairs – Toohey and Catherine, Alinsky and Clinton – though not to the exclusion of the political aspects of the relationships.

First, here is a description of Catherine Halsey when she is introduced in *The Fountainhead*, and, incidentally, into Ellsworth Toohey's life:

> "Toohey had not intended to keep her in his own home. But when she stepped off the train in New York, her plain little face looked beautiful for a moment, as if the future were opening before her and its glow were already upon her forehead, as if she were eager and proud and ready to meet it. It was one of those rare moments when the humblest person knows suddenly what it means to feel as the center of the universe, and is made beautiful by the knowledge, and the world – in the eyes of witnesses – looks like a better place for having such a center. Ellsworth Toohey saw this – and decided that Catherine would

remain with him." (*The Fountainhead*, pp. 310-311, Centennial Edition).

In subsequent scenes that feature Catherine Halsey, she is depicted as having a self that struggles to understand the world and her uncle, a self that progressively loses the struggle under her uncle's malicious guidance. She is intellectually unarmed to defend herself against Toohey's attacks, which are aimed at *disarming* her mind by denigrating it and her values. Her sole consolation or value in this period is Peter Keating and her love for him.

When Keating abandons her to marry Dominique Francon – an action encouraged by Toohey for his own malign ends – Catherine collapses spiritually. That is the last we see of her until much later in the novel (Part 4: Howard Roark, Chapter 10, pp. 621-628). Here is how Peter Keating, who once wanted to marry her, sees her after years of being out of contact:

"…But when he lifted his eyes to Catherine, he knew that no caution was necessary; she did not react to his scrutiny; her expression remained the same, whether he studied her face or that of the woman at the next table; she seemed to have no consciousness of her own person.

> "It was her mouth that had changed most, he thought; the lips were drawn in, with only a pale edge of flesh left around the imperious line of their opening; a mouth to issue orders, he thought, but not big orders or cruel orders; just mean little ones – about plumbing and disinfectants. He saw the fine wrinkles at the corners of her eyes – a skin like paper that had been crumpled and then smoothed out."

When Keating asks her what she felt when he failed to elope with her and when she learned that he was married to Dominique, that is, if she suffered, Catherine answers:

> "Yes, of course I suffered. All young people do in such situations. It seems foolish afterward. I cried, and I screamed some dreadful things at Uncle Ellsworth, and he had to call a doctor to give me a sedative, and then weeks afterward I fainted on the street one day without any reason, which was really disgraceful. All the conventional things, I suppose, everybody goes through them, like measles. Why should I have expected to be exempt? – as Uncle Ellsworth said."

At this point, even Keating, who himself has not only betrayed her and everything else he might have valued, is appalled by the dead, utter selflessness of Catherine. She has become what Toohey intended her to be, an interchangeable manqué, in her own eyes no better or no worse than anyone else, a person who finds "self worth" only in serving others, or the public good. She has become a humorless, miniature clone of Toohey. Instead of aiming for control of the country's political life and directing it to collectivism, Catherine is satisfied with overseeing "plumbing and disinfectants" as a government social worker.

And the world was no longer a better place for the glow on her forehead. That glow had been methodically extinguished by Toohey.

"Plumbing and disinfectants" best describes Saul Alinsky's brand of Toohey-ism. His whole political philosophy was definably collectivist. It was Marxism wearing a plastic Halloween mask. For all her adulation of him, Hillary was not satisfied with the range of Alinsky's achievements in the political realm. They were, to her, not ambitious enough. He advocated merely "activism" on the part of the poor and ethnic to achieve "social justice," and organizing "communities" or neighborhoods to engage the "establishment" in direct conflict. However, he thought in terms of groups.

Lessons were to be learned from Alinsky by young Hillary.

The ultimate goal of such groups, he wrote, was to acquire power. He had the hubris to rank himself as "radical" as Thomas Jefferson, Thomas Paine, and Patrick Henry, overlooking the fact that these men advocated liberty and individualism in their political philosophy. Alinsky advocated rule by chain gangs and mobs via "democracy" – which in the Left's lexicon is a euphemism for socialism or collectivism.

Hillary Clinton quotes Alinsky from his book, *Reveille for Radicals,* published in 1946:

> "What does the Radical want? He wants a world in which the worth of the individual is recognized...a world based on the morality of mankind...The Radical believes that all peoples should have a high standard of food, housing, and health....The Radical places human rights far above property rights. He is for universal, free public education and recognizes this as fundamental to the democratic way of life...."

But, all this was government policy by the time Hillary wrote her thesis. She even acknowledges it in the paragraph immediately following the quotation:

> "Much of what Alinsky professes does not sound 'radical.' His are the words used in our schools and churches, by our parents and their friends, by our peers. The difference is that Alinsky really believes in them and recognizes the necessity of changing the present structures of our lives in order to realize them."

Alinsky's means for attaining "social justice" is for groups to mobilize to achieve power, for power can "compel negotiations." Only by "organizing" can otherwise powerless and voiceless groups win concessions from the "establishment." In an article cited by Hillary, Alinsky asserted that,

> "We have become involved in bypaths of confusion or semantics…The word 'power' has through time acquired overtones of sinister corrupt evil, unhealthy immoral Machiavellianism, and a general phantasmagoria of the nether regions." Hillary comments, with implicit approval, "For Alinsky, power is the 'very essence of life, the dynamic of life' and is found in '…active citizen participation pulsing upward providing a unified strength for a common purpose of organization…either changing circumstances or opposing change."

The speech that reflects the spirit and contains the germs of everything that Alinsky advocated is on page 103 of *The Fountainhead*, when, during a building-trades union strike in New York, Toohey addresses a hall of strike supporters:

> "…The lesson to be learned from our tragic struggle is the lesson of unity. We shall unite or we shall be defeated. Our will – the will of the disinherited, the forgotten, the oppressed – shall weld us into a solid bulwark, with a common faith and a common goal. This is the time for every man to renounce the thoughts of his petty little problems, of gain, of comfort, of self-gratification. This is the time to merge his self in a great current, in the rising tide which is approaching to sweep us all, willing or unwilling, into the future. History, my friends, does not ask questions or acquiescence. It is irrevocable, as the voice of the masses that determine it. Let us listen to the call. Let us organize, my brothers. Let us organize. Let us organize. Let us organize."

This was Alinsky's credo in a nutshell, a perfect encapsulation of his means and ends. It is doubtful that Ayn Rand had even heard of Alinsky while she was writing *The Fountainhead* – his first book, *Reveille for Radicals* did not appear until three years after publication of *The Fountainhead* – but Hillary certainly had read her novels while in college (as a passing "phase," as has been reported elsewhere). If she was lost in the "bypaths of confusion and semantics" – searching for a "cause" that would sanction her own life and give it direction – one can imagine that she would reject the notion that Toohey was a villain. She would have been as impressed with Toohey's ideology and methodology as she was with Alinsky's, but with fewer reservations.

The important point here is that Alinsky remains one of her primary ideological mentors, her denials and those of her defenders to the contrary notwithstanding. Her career after leaving Yale Law School was a frantic scramble to find a way to enter politics.

Carl Bernstein, who wrote a biography of Hillary, *A Woman in Charge*, in a July 20th interview with Jon Wiener on the *Truthdig* site, claims that she is not an ideologue of the collectivist or any other stripe.

> "One of the real problems Hillary has had is a difficult relationship with the truth....One of the things she's been most truthful about is that she's not easy to compartmentalize in terms of ideology."

But the power hungry *do* subscribe to an ideology of sorts, one of opportunism, of snatching at every issue or chance that would boost one's place in the political power grid. Hillary found that opportunity in Bill Clinton, himself a consummate opportunist, whom she met at Yale. She rode on his political coattails all the way to the White House. She miscalculated when, as the power behind the Oval Office, she attempted to maneuver Congress into adopting full-scale socialized health care.

Whether she was slavishly working to apply Alinsky's rules of thumb, to work both from "within" and "without" the system," to effect change by organized confrontation, or adhering to some other leftist ideologue's formula for acquiring power, is a moot issue. It is interesting to note that during Bill Clinton's two administrations, Hillary's Wellesley thesis was kept locked up by the school at the request of the White House, doubtless to prevent the public from getting the "wrong" ideas concerning her ideological leanings. But her actions before and since have tipped everyone off to her true leanings. The school did not need to keep her thesis a secret.

The London *Daily Telegraph* of August 7 reported Republican candidate Rudy Giuliani as saying that Hillary "wouldn't admit she's a liberal." He made the remark when Hillary recently "disavowed the label and said she was a 'modern progressive.'" One wonders what distinction there is between an old and a "modern" progressive. The labels "liberal" and "progressive" are virtually synonymous, and simply stand for the incremental creep towards a total welfare state.

In her thesis, Hillary seems to have mastered the sociological jargon necessary for anyone thinking of dedicating his life to "public service." In one paragraph, she writes:

> "Societal comparisons raise again questions about the meaning of 'radical' and even 'revolutionary' within a mass production/consumption state, particularly the United States. Must definitions perhaps be as fluid as the actions they purport to describe?....Alinsky would answer affirmatively."

So would Hillary. It presages her future husband's retort of what the meaning of "is" is. Bill and Hillary were and would remain soul-mates.

On July 29, the *New York Times* ran an article about Hillary's college year letters to a high school classmate, John Peavoy ("In the '60s, a Future Candidate Poured Her Heart Out in Letters"). What is most interesting about the letters the article discusses is that they reveal how emotion-driven she was in choosing her ultimate politics. Upon entering Wellesley, she morphed from being a Goldwater Republican and a member of the Young Republicans to a volunteer for Eugene McCarthy's antiwar presidential campaign.

No doubt her intellectual and moral rudderlessness made her susceptible to the antiwar rhetoric and activism of the period. This was also the period in which she discovered Saul Alinsky and his brand of activism.

I don't think a glow of the future ever graced Hillary's forehead. Catherine Halsey had a more adult and advanced sense of her self and what was possible to her than Hillary evidently had at the same age. No eagerness or pride is evident in Hillary's letters or her thesis, just a kind of inverse narcissism, or a concern for what she thinks of herself through others' eyes. In one of her letters to Peavoy, she remarks that she has "not yet reconciled myself to the fate of not being the star."

By page 375 of *The Fountainhead,* Catherine is experiencing a personal crisis over her social work and turns to her uncle for guidance. "I have no selfish desire left, I have nothing of my own – and I'm miserable." She tells Toohey that she has grown to hate the poor who depend on her.

Toohey tells her that her problem is that she expected to feel virtuous and personally happy for "doing right," and that this was vicious and egotistical.

She replies, "But if you have no…no self-respect, how can you be anything?"

Toohey tells her that she must stop wanting *anything.* "You must forget how important Miss Catherine Halsey is. Because, you see, she isn't. Men are important only in relation to other men, in their usefulness, in the service they render….You must be willing to suffer, to be cruel, to be dishonest, to be unclean – anything, my dear, anything to kill the most stubborn of roots, the ego. And only when it is dead, when you care no longer, when you have lost your identity and forgotten the name of your soul – only then will you know the kind of happiness I spoke about, and the gates of spiritual grandeur will fall open before you."

"But, Uncle Ellsworth," she whispered, "when the gates fall open, who is it that's going to enter?"

Toohey, momentarily surprised by the perceptiveness of her question – he knows it was an important rebuttal, but she does not – replies with a put-down about her having made a "smart crack." Catherine, intimidated by his "wisdom" and utterly ignorant of its nature, concedes. Alinsky and Toohey agreed that "Ridicule is man's most potent weapon." (Alinsky enunciated it in his *Rules for Radicals* [1971]; Toohey expounded on it to Peter Keating in Part 4, Chapter 16, p. 665.)

Compare that with Hillary's quest for the meaning of her life in her letters to Peavoy. One letter to him she signs "Me," parenthetically adding "the world's saddest word." That one brief signature can stand to represent the self-deprecatory remarks in all her other letters discussed by the *Times*. I do not think Hillary suffered from a crisis of self-respect, as Catherine Halsey did; I do not think she ever had a self to respect. She would have agreed with everything Toohey told Catherine, without Toohey having to exert much effort to convince her or having to resort to vicious put-downs.

It takes a village, or a Toohey, or an Alinsky, to fill such a void. This is a candidate for the Presidency of the United States. Hillary has progressed from doubting the effectiveness of massive government programs to help the poor to seeing them as the only answer, in the name of "social justice." Like Alinsky, like Toohey, she wishes to crush the individualist independence of Americans and replace it with dependence on the state – and she would *be* the state – chiefly because she has grown to fear and hate independence in anyone.

No matter how slickly "human" she presents her made-over self to the public in debates or during interviews, one can still detect in her the desire to kill in every American his integrity, self-respect, sense of values, the heroic, and happiness. When she left Wellesley, she decided to become the "star," someone whom uncounted others would come to depend on and thank for that dependence.

This is a would-be dictator, and dictators, as I have noted in other commentaries, are only as real to themselves as the number of people they need to rule and command.

When Keating abandons her to marry Dominique Francon – an action encouraged by Toohey for his own malign ends – Catherine collapses spiritually.

This actually is not the last we see of Catherine Halsey. She reappears briefly on p. 398 (in the Centennial Edition of *The Fountainhead*). Through Ellsworth Toohey's influence, she is given a position in charge of occupational therapy in the Hopton Stoddard Home for Subnormal Children – Roark's vandalized Stoddard Temple. She is depicted as being ecstatic when "the least promising" of the children exhibits signs of intelligence or an awareness of reality.

Ayn Rand may have implied that Toohey meant the "occupational therapy" to be for Catherine herself, as a kind of finishing touch to his malevolent handiwork – finishing in the sense that such a job would complete the destruction of her identity and even corrupt her measure of "normalcy," in herself and in others. What she says about the "art" produced by the genderless Jackie is, ironically, what she never heard from her uncle Ellsworth or anyone else when she attempted to apprehend reality.

That whole section on the Home, on pages 395 to 398, also underscores Toohey's value-destroying methodology, in this instance the conversion of a temple to the human spirit into a clinic for the contemplation of the irrational and the diseased.

Also, I neglected to mention another thing that Hillary Clinton fears and which she would wish to bypass in Americans through statist legislation (or force): the element of volition. The volition (implied in the concept of independence) of individuals would confound any of her well-laid plans to impose mandatory compliance with her wishes (or the wishes of virtually any politician, for that matter). Further, she would want all Americans to become public service drudges in spirit, if not in fact.

August 2007

The Liberal/Left's Ventriloquist Dummy

Former President Bill Clinton revealed his totalitarian bent during an interview with ABC's Jake Tapper on April 17, when he linked Timothy McVeigh and the Oklahoma City bombing of a federal building in 1995 with current "anti-government" rhetoric, rallies and demonstrations by Tea Partiers. It is almost surreal, listening to this vile, hypocritical, amoral person pontificating on the necessity for civil debate. His language was banal, but in its banality, lurked evil.

One can't decide if Clinton was speaking *ad libitum* or reciting a memorized lesson. It sounded like a rehearsed spiel. Perhaps it was a teleprompter he was reading over Tapper's shoulder, out of camera shot. His focus was on "demonization" he said can motivate people to commit atrocious crimes. He is a product of the Frankfurt social engineering school of politics: men have no real volition, they are just products of their social and economic environment, and not really responsible for their values or actions — until, mysteriously, a force compels them to make a choice and turn to violence or to utter nasty things about their perceived oppressors.

Except, of course, if they happen to be leftists, Democratic flunkies, the Students for a Democratic Society, Bill Ayers, Reverend Jeremiah Wright, and a large company of enemies of capitalism, individual rights, limited government, and civil debate. Then, violence is okay. They're on the side of the totalitarians and social engineers in government. Their "demonization" and "careless language" are forgiven when by chance they're remembered.

The Frankfurt School, as readers might remember, was an institution that promoted communism and socialism and heavily influenced especially American academia in virtually all the humanities. Banned in Germany by Hitler, it moved to the U.S. and established the New School for Social Research in New York. It reestablished itself in Germany after the war.

If the Frankfurt School acted as the theoretical arm of socialist/fascist advocacy, Saul Alinsky, Hillary Clinton's mentor in political action, was its most prominent field agent.

Clinton himself was the Progressive heir to John F. Kennedy. I have kept for years a New York Times full-page photo of 17-year-old Bill Clinton, then a member of the American Legion Boys Club, shaking hands with JFK in the White House Rose Garden in July 1963. I dubbed the photo "Passing the Torch of Fascism." I kept it to remind me of the link between Clinton's polices and JFK's and how those policies, if not questioned and throttled, would continue to be implemented and expanded under Republicans and Democrats alike in the future. During his two terms as president, Clinton and his wife worked to advance statism. According to one fawning article:

Clinton was one of the first in line to shake President Kennedy's hand in the Rose Garden. That event was one of the most important experiences of his youth. After that, he knew he wanted to make a difference in the lives of the people of America by becoming President of the United States.

Again, listening to Clinton ramble on about the consequences of "violence-provoking" rhetoric like a cracker-barrel yahoo in the backwaters of Arkansas, one cannot believe this person is emblematic of the forces that have been working to convert the vestiges of a constitutional republic into a European style socialist "republic" governed by an elective and appointive political elite.

However, a scrutiny of the moral and intellectual depths and make-up of most of our current political leaders — including Republicans, but especially of the ones in power now, the Democrats — leaves one the poorer for the effort. They are neither sinister nor brilliant; they exhibit no evidence of being "evil geniuses." They are "ordinary" in the sense that they are non-intellectual opportunists taking advantage of an absence of reason in politics, a phenomenon of which they are not aware. They are the cockroaches, poisonous centipedes, and maggots who can infest an unoccupied house. There. I've demonized Pelosi, Frank, Reid and many more. So, sue me, Bill.

In answer to Tapper's question about Rush Limbaugh's charge that, because of a speech Clinton gave about the 15th anniversary of the Oklahoma City bombing by McVeigh, Clinton would be responsible for future violence, Clinton answered:

> The only point I tried to make is that when I went back and started preparing for the 15th anniversary of Oklahoma City, I realized that there were a lot of parallels between the early '90s and now, both in the feeling of economic dislocation, and the level of uncertainty people felt. The rise of kind of identity politics. The rise of the militia movements and the right wing talk radio with a lot of what's going on in the blogosphere now.

That was his opening remark. What an invitation to regulate the Internet.

And in the right wing media, and with Oath Keepers, the 3 percenters, the — all these people, you know, who are saying things like, "If Idaho wants to succeed from the union," the militia group out there says, you know, "We'll back them." One leader of one of these groups said that all politics was just a prelude to civil war. And then the politicians of course have not been that serious, but a lot of the things that have been said, they — they create a climate in which people who are vulnerable to violence because they are disoriented like Timothy McVeigh was are more likely to act.

And the only point I tried to make was that we ought to have a lot of political dissent — a lot of political argument. Nobody is right all the time. But we also have to take responsibility for the possible consequences of what we say. And we shouldn't demonize the government or its public employees or its elected officials. We can disagree with them. We can harshly criticize them. But when we turn them into an object of demonization, you know, you — you increase the number of threats. But I worry about these threats against the president and the Congress. And I worry about more careless language even against — some of which we've seen against the Republican governor in New Jersey, Governor Christie.

As Tony Blankley in Real Clear Politics and Philip Klein in American Spectator note in their incisive articles, this is the "same old, same old" from Clinton's Alinskyite playbook: check anyone who voices anti-big-government ideas and criticisms by demonizing them in return with suggestions of "probable" violence, sedition, insurrection, or otherwise disturbing the public peace.

Bethania Assy, in her essay on Hannah Arendt's book, *Eichmann in Jerusalem*, reports on Arendt's surprise by how innocuous Adolf Eichmann looked.

Hannah Arendt's first reaction to Eichmann, "the man in the glass booth," was — *nicht einmal unheimlich* — not even sinister." She argues that "The deeds were monstrous, but the doer ... was quite ordinary, commonplace, and neither demonic nor monstrous." Arendt's perception that Eichmann seemed to be a common man, evidenced in his transparent superficiality and mediocrity, left her astonished in measuring the unaccounted evil committed by him, that is, organizing the deportation of millions of Jews to the concentration camps. Actually, what Arendt had detected in Eichmann was not even stupidity, in her words, he portrayed something entirely negative, it was *thoughtlessness*. Eichmann's ordinariness implied in an incapacity for independent critical thought: "... the only specific characteristic one could detect in his past as well as in his behavior during the trial and the preceding police examination was something entirely negative: it was not stupidity but a curious, quite *authentic inability to think*."

This is not to suggest that Clinton is or could have become another Eichmann; rather, it is to know that Clinton's banality — and that of countless other "ordinary" individuals who have never had an original thought in their entire lives and don't intend to — makes possible the kinds of crimes a demonic or monstrous Eichmann could commit. Think of all the political non-entities in Weimar and Nazi Germany whose public pronouncements on politics are forgotten, but whose words helped to move countless thoughtless Germans in the direction of the Third Reich. Clinton, as contemptuous of America as his current successor in office, simply repeated the smear against opposition to Obama's policies launched by the left and the Democrats. It was indeed a thoughtless iteration of the same charge, solicited by Tapper, a "journalist" far down in the ranks of those who want to believe, rather than think.

Thoughtless? Yes, to the extent that Clinton did not need to remember anything but what he has been told, taught, and was expected to repeat all his life — and has never questioned. In this instance, on cue from Tapper, he merely weaved the same old bromides and catch phrases of the left into his homey delivery of an answer. He did not need — and certainly didn't feel the need to — to look reflective and check his words, and reply something to the effect:

> "Well, you know, all the bad things being said about the Tea Party and Americans being worried about the government, that's unfair, because none of the people I saw on TV looked like they were about to blow up buildings like Timothy McVeigh did in Oklahoma City, I don't think these people are disturbed in the way McVeigh was. I think that's a disgraceful accusation and someone ought to apologize for it. They looked like ordinary, angry Americans who think they're getting a raw deal from the government, so, who can blame them? I don't agree with anything they've said, but they should be allowed to say it without being called racists or bigots or Nazis."

That's what Clinton could have said. But didn't. And couldn't. He has been credited with being a shrewd politician, able to play sides against each other and come out the winner. But, is that *thought*, or is it merely the feral instincts of a predator, who "thinks" in terms of pressure points, favors, slander, extortion, arm-twisting, personalities, deceit, fraud, and gaming a corrupt system?

Why was Clinton asked for his thoughts? Because the Left has been searching desperately for an "official" sanction of their unrelenting smear campaign against Americans who oppose the take-over of their lives and wealth by Obama and Congress. And they chose, not so ironically, "Grand Old

Man" Bill Clinton, a creature only a little less vile, hypocritical, amoral, power-lusting, and slickly dissimulating than his current successor in the Oval Office. Or, rather, "they" didn't choose him; he simply fell into line, as did Tapper. Birds of a feather.

Was Tapper part of a conspiracy? Was he asked to solicit Clinton's all-too-predictable opinion? No. It was just part of the liberal political culture in which Tapper resides. It was as natural for him to pose the question to Clinton as it would be for a priest to query the Pope on a theological matter.

Clinton represents the Left's conception of a respectable, "disinterested" third-party concurring in his own distinctive style with the notion that "angry rhetoric" and "careless language" pose a threat of violence, and with Obama's growl that Tea Party dissension should be "toned down."

The hypocrisy of Clinton, the Democrats, and the Left is the least serious charge one could lay on them. Clinton's political record is so rife with corruption and underhanded political manipulation it doesn't need recounting here. I suspect that he deliberately sabotaged his wife's bid for the Democratic nomination in hopes of foisting Obama on the country; I refuse to believe he is so stupid and gauche to say the things he said during her campaign without meaning his statements to have some consequence. Perhaps that was his vengeance on her and on the country that nominally rejected his and her socialist policies when Al Gore's bid for power went down in flames in 2000.

The Clinton marriage has always been one of political convenience; I do not think they see each other much, with Bill traveling hither and yon collecting munificent speaking fees and playing the humanitarian, and Hillary globe-trotting doing Obama's bidding to betray our allies and make friends of tin pot tyrants. That's her vengeance on the country that rejected her. I believe this conjecture is valid, founded on the characters and whorish behavior of both Clintons in their quest for power.

It is unfortunate that the Democrats and leftists have appropriated the term "demonization." But, I refuse to argue the issue on the enemy's terms. A *demon*, after all, is either an evil spirit intent on causing mischief, or it's a tormenting anxiety about something. Americans certainly see the Obama agenda as inherently evil and promising nothing but mischief, and they're right to be anxious to the point of torment that the agenda means them no good.

Minnesota representative Michele Bachmann, to whom Clinton referred when he remarked that some politicians "create a climate in which people who are vulnerable to violence are disoriented," for example, did not "demonize" the Obama administration and Congress by calling it a "gangster government." She *characterized* it, by correctly identifying the key features and consequences of legislative fraud (and gave columnist Michael Barone credit for coining the term; has any Democrat or administration official given

Saul Alinsky credit for the smear tactic? They don't dare.). Then, it was merely the consequences of the government take-over of General Motors. As it is clear now to anyone with two eyes and a functioning mind — a mind that is willing to see the ample evidence and is willing to think — the term can be applied to the whole of Obama's administration.

Bill Clinton is a minor but prominent player in the ongoing debacle. His words on the Tea Party and talk radio and Timothy McVeigh were intended to elevate a disgusting smear campaign from blatantly obvious turpitude to the level of righteous moral concern. He opened his mouth and scurrilous words came from it.

We have heard all he said before — from President Barack Obama, from Nancy Pelosi, from Harry Reid, from Barney Frank, from the New York Times and the Washington Post, and the MSM — and those are the voices we heard when Bill Clinton spoke.

He sits on the liberal/left lap, and others move his mouth. Mortimer Snerd, anyone?

April 2010

§   **The End**   §

.